The Complete Barbecue Cookbook

The Complete Barbecue Cookbook

Recipes for the Gas Grill and Water Smoker

Charmglow®

Contemporary Books, Inc.
Chicago

Library of Congress Cataloging in Publication Data

Main entry under title:

The complete barbecue cookbook.

   Includes index.
   1. Barbecue cookery.
TX840.B3C65   1983   641.5'784   83-1897
ISBN 0-8092-5554-5
ISBN 0-8092-5553-7 (pbk.)

All recipes have been tested by Charlotte Erickson, noted Food and Appliance Consultant. She is also author of *The Freezer Cookbook* and *Shortcut Cooking*, published by Contemporary Books. Ms. Erickson is an active lecturer and cooking demonstrator in the greater Chicago and northern Illinois areas.

Photographs on pages 30, 36, 37, and 123 courtesy of National Live Stock and Meat Board. Photograph on page 70 courtesy of State of Florida Department of Natural Resources. Line drawings courtesy of Reynolds Aluminum.

First Contemporary trade paperback edition 1984

Copyright © 1983 by Charmglow Products, Division Beatrice Foods Co.
All rights reserved
Published by Contemporary Books, Inc.
180 North Michigan Avenue, Chicago, Illinois 60601
Manufactured in the United States of America
Library of Congress Catalog Card Number: 83-1897
International Standard Book Number: 0-8092-5554-5 (cloth)
                                                    0-8092-5553-7 (paper)

Published simultaneously in Canada by Beaverbooks, Ltd.
195 Allstate Parkway, Valleywood Business Park
Markham, Ontario L3R 4T8 Canada

Contents

Introduction		vii
How to Cook with Your Gas Grill	**1**	1
Marinades and Sauces	**2**	15
Appetizers	**3**	25
Meats	**4**	33
Poultry	**5**	55
Fish and Seafood	**6**	65
Vegetables and Fruits	**7**	77
Hamburgers, Hot Dogs, Sandwiches, and Breads	**8**	89
Wok Cooking	**9**	107
Smoker Cooking	**10**	117
Appendix: Party Calculator		139
Index		145

Introduction

Barbecuing in America has come of age. What started a few decades ago as a frustrating backyard battle between cook and a smoking charcoal inferno has been refined into a sophisticated culinary art.

This art is as American as baseball and apple pie. It's also as classic as fine French cooking. When done properly barbecue cooking has no peer for versatility, flavor excellence, and colorful presentation.

In fact, barbecuing today has become a way of life for many Americans. Cooking *al fresco* has appeal all year long. Appetites abound at the sight and aroma of meats, fresh vegetables, and seasoned breads.

As barbecue cooking has improved, so has barbecue equipment. The greatest advancement since the charcoal briquet was Charmglow's introduction of the gas-fired barbecue grill. Restaurant chefs long have charbroiled steaks over grills incorporating gas flame-heated briquets. After all, chefs knew that it was the burning fat that imparted the barbecue flavor to foods, not the charcoal.

Drawing on chefs' knowledge, Charmglow designed a variety of grills using gas to heat permanent pumice briquets. Bettering the restaurant grill, Charmglow added a hinged lid, thus allowing the cook to control heat better, cook in wind or bad weather, and still achieve the same flavor of smoke cookery.

Constantly improved designs of both burners and controls have brought to the modern barbecue cook all the conveniences of cooking on a kitchen range. Gone are problems of flame-ups and excess smoke. Foods cook to perfection over the proper heat, controlled by turning a dial. Cleanup is easy, as the Charmglow grill virtually cleans itself.

With all this convenience, the cook can now spend more time with family or guests. Many Charmglow grill owners find that their barbecue often is the life of the party. In fact, it can be the star attraction if a variety of uncooked foods are set out and guests are invited to do their own thing with skewers, sauces, and spices. The number of cooking experiences are endless, considering the variety of cart and stationary models, the accessories and attachments ranging from electric spits to baskets.

What makes barbecuing unique is the cook. Given the proper equipment and guidance, there is no limit to how fancy or individualized the result will be. This book covers the basic foods most enjoyed in America. Although it is written with sufficient clarity for the beginner or novice chef, its recipes will add a new dimension to the most experienced barbecue enthusiast. There are endless variations using different marinades, herbs, and spices. But this collection of recipes does include a number of ethnic flavors and regional favorites, along with most of the traditional barbecue foods Americans cook regularly.

By adding your own personal touch to your Charmglow cooking, you can be proud of the results every time.

How to Cook with Your Gas Grill

1

Cooking with a gas grill is easy and fun; it's just like having a complete stove outside. It has the versatility of being movable and can be used near your kitchen door and/or on your patio, whatever the occasion demands. No need to heat up your kitchen with your stove; your gas grill can do it all. Casseroles, breads, and other baked or roasted dishes can be cooked on your grill by using indirect heat or the warming shelf. Cooking your complete meal on the grill eliminates a lot of running back and forth from the patio to the kitchen. It saves electricity as well, which is particularly important when your house air conditioning units are being used.

GETTING ACQUAINTED WITH YOUR GRILL

Be sure to read your owner's manual for instructions on seasoning the grill for first-time use, on flame adjustment, and on cleaning your grill. Because of differences in climate—temperatures and/or wind conditions—time and cooking temperatures will vary somewhat depending on where you live.

The best way to become familiar with temperature variations in your particular area is to use an oven thermometer and record the internal temperatures on your grill when it is set on medium, low, and with the top partially opened and closed. Wind conditions will also be a considerable factor in these readings. If your grill is in a protected area, wind may not be a factor; however, it isn't always possible to pick such a site.

Wind conditions differ widely across the country, as does altitude. It is difficult to predict how your grill is going to cook in your particular area without testing it first. The following chart gives the temperatures produced by a Charmglow grill tested in the Midwest at approximately 50° F. at a 500-foot altitude. If your temperatures read higher or lower, you can adjust cooking time accordingly. Compare the temperatures of your grill with the temperature on the following chart (record yours in the space provided).

Your grill temperatures can easily be increased or decreased. Some models have a lid adjustment handle that can easily prop the grill lid open in a one-, two-, or three-inch position. For models that do not have this adjustment device we recommend using a wooden-handled utensil for this purpose. On the large deluxe grill, temperature can be increased by using two burners at a low setting instead of one.

Direct cooking occurs when nothing is between the food and the gas flames except the grid. Indirect cooking for one- or two-burner grills includes all rotisserie cooking, the use of foil and metal pans, and any cooking done on a roasting rack with a foil drip pan. On two-burner units with only one burner lit, indirect cooking also occurs when foods are grilled on the unlighted half of the grill.

Two-Burner Grill

Gas grills come with one or two gas burners, located on the bottom of the grill cavity. Two burners provide a larger area for indirect cooking, as well as more temperature variation.

One-Burner Grill

The single-burner gas grill can be adapted to the same methods of cooking as the two-burner model. Indirect cooking can be performed on the warming shelf. You can also line half of the cooking grid with a double thickness of heavy-duty foil or use a large foil baking pan over half the cooking surface. This covered half of your grill will have the same cooking effect as the unlighted side of a two-burner grill. To ensure even cooking temperatures on your grill, be sure that your briquets are spread evenly in a single layer over your burners. These briquets absorb the gas heat and radiate it to your food on the grill.

TEMPERATURE CONTROL

Grill temperatures can easily be controlled. If, for instance, your food is cooking too fast and your control setting is on low, open the lid one or two inches, depending on the amount of heat reduction you desire. For more heat, close the lid and turn both burners on.

High

The high setting is used primarily to preheat the briquets for no more than five minutes before grilling starts. It may also be used for quick searing of meats, especially steaks cooked rare, and wok cooking. But rarely, if ever, will you do any extended cooking on the high setting. High heat also aids in cleaning grids with the lid closed after cooking. Do not leave the grill while cleaning is in process. Clean often to avoid grease fires.

With the lid closed, the cooking temperature at the grill level will exceed 650° F. *Searing meat quickly at high temperatures seals in the juices and is recommended for roasts and steaks.*

Medium

Medium is used for open grill cooking such as preparing Bananas Flambé and Cherries Jubilee (see recipes) and doing other such cooking. It may also be used for searing thin cuts of meat. With the lid closed and both burners turned on, the cooking temperature at grill level will exceed 500° F.

Low

Most barbecue foods should be cooked at low. Even thick steaks that have been seared on both sides at high or medium will finish with better texture and more juices at low. All roasts and rotisserie foods should be cooked on low. With the lid closed, no wind, and one burner

Temperature Chart for One Burner

GRILL MODEL	LOW (F.)	YOUR TEMPERATURE
Small Grill with Window	375°	_____
Large Deluxe	310°	_____
Small Grill without Window	400°	_____

turned on, the cooking temperature at grill level should be between 310° F. and 400° F., depending on the model. With two burners on low, the temperature range is between 570° F. and 650° F. Casserole cooking or baking with the indirect cooking method should be done with the lid closed.

COOKING METHODS

Indirect Cooking

Two Burner Model

This is always done with the lid down and is essentially the equivalent of roasting or baking. Food is cooked by circulating hot air all around the food. The food has no smoke flavor, as no smoke is created unless you add wet hickory or fruit woods. Indirect cooking can be done on the warming shelf while using the direct method on the lower grids. On the two-burner gas grill indirect heating can be done as follows: Heat both sides of your grill on high for five minutes. Turn off the gas on one side and turn the temperature down, usually to low on the other side. Place food on the side of the grill that has been shut off and close the grill lid quickly to minimize heat loss.

A stronger barbecue flavor can be given to foods that need slow and/or indirect cooking by searing the food on medium for two or three minutes per side with the lid closed. Finish cooking the food on the unlit side. Remember to shorten the total cooking time accordingly.

Single Burner Model

Line half of the cooking grid with a double thickness of heavy-duty foil or use a large foil baking pan over half the cooking surface. This covered half of your grill will have the same cooking effect as the unlighted side of a two-burner grill.

Direct Cooking

This is the most common method used for grilling steaks, chops, burgers, sausages, and kabobs. Food is placed on the cooking grids directly over the permanent pumice briquets. As the fat from the meat drips onto the briquets, it smokes, permeating your meat with a natural smoky flavor.

The following table lists cooking times and methods for various meats, poultry, and seafood, cooked by the direct or indirect technique. It can be used to cook on both one-burner and two-burner grills.

Gas Grilling Chart

Meat	Size or Weight	Heat Control	Time
BEEF			
Roasts			
Beef Chuck/in foil (well done)	3–5 lbs.	Low/lid closed/indirect	1¼ hrs.
Rolled Rump (boneless)—med.-rare		Low/lid closed/direct	23 min. per lb.
Rolled Rib Roast—med.-rare		Low/lid closed/indirect (rotisserie)	14 min. per lb.
Rolled Rib Roast—med.-rare		Low/lid closed/indirect (roasting rack)	17 min. per lb.

How to Cook with Your Gas Grill

Meat	Size or Weight	Heat Control	Time
Sirloin Tip		Low/lid closed/indirect (rotisserie)	23 min. per lb.
Rolled Sirloin Tip—med.-rare		Low/lid closed/indirect (roasting rack)	26 min. per lb.
Steaks			
(T-Bone, Porterhouse, Sirloin, Strip, and other cuts)	Rare—		
	½" thick	Low/lid closed/direct	1 min. (30 sec. per side)
	1" thick	Low/lid closed/direct	6 min. (3 min. per side)
	1½" thick	Low/lid closed/direct	7 min. (3½ min. per side)
	1¾–2" thick	Sear on high low/	4 min. (2 min. per side)
		Continue on low Lid closed/direct	14 min. (7 min. per side)
	Med.-Rare—		
	½" thick	Low/lid closed/direct	2 min. (1 min. per side)
	1" thick	Low/lid closed/direct	7 min. (3½ min. per side)
	1½" thick	Low/lid closed/direct	8 min. (4 min. per side)
	1¾–2" thick	Sear on high	4 min. (2 min. per side)
		Continue on low Lid closed/direct	20 min. (10 min. per side)
	Med.-Well—		
	½" thick	Low/lid closed/direct	3 min. (1½ min. per side)
	1" thick	Low/lid closed/direct	8 min. (4 min. per side)
	1½" thick	Low/lid closed/direct	9 min. (4½ min. per side)
	1¾–2" thick	Low/lid closed/direct	13 min. (6½ min. per side)
Fillets	Rare—½" thick	Low/lid closed/direct	4 min. (2 min. per side)
	Med.-Rare—½" thick	Low/lid closed/direct	8 min. (4 min. per side)
Butt Steak	Rare—1–1¼" thick	Sear on high	4 min. (2 min. per side)
		Continue on low Lid closed/direct	2 min. (1 min. per side)
Cube Steak	Med.-Well	High/lid closed/direct	4 min. (2 min. per side)
Flank Steak	Med.-Rare—1" thick	Low/lid closed/direct	16 min. (8 min. per side)
Minute Steak	Med.-Well—¼–½" thick	High/lid closed/direct	4 min. (2 min. per side)
Salisbury Steak	Well Done—¼" thick	Low/lid closed/direct	8 min (4 min. per side)
Top Round Steak	Rare—2" thick	Sear on high	12 min. (6 min. per side, turning several times)
		Continue on low Lid closed/direct	10 min. (5 min. per side, turning several times)
	Med.-Rare—2" thick	Sear on high	12 min. (6 min. per side)
		Continue on low Lid closed/direct	11 min. (5½ min. per side, turning several times)
	Well Done— 2" thick	Low/lid closed/direct	12 min. (6 min. per side)
Top Sirloin	2–3" thick	High/lid closed/direct	4 min. (2 min. per side)

Meat	Size or Weight	Heat Control	Time
Hamburgers			
Rare	1" thick–¼ lbs.	Low/lid closed/direct	4 min. (2 min. per side)
Med.-Rare		Low/lid closed/direct	5 min. (2½ min. per side)
Med.-Well		Low/lid closed/direct	6 min. (3 min. per side)
Well Done		Low/lid closed/direct	8 min. (4 min. per side)
Corned Beef		Low/lid closed/direct	15 min. per lb.
LAMB			
Crown Roast of Lamb—Med.-Rare	4–5 lbs.	Low/lid closed/direct	20 min. per lb.
Leg of Lamb (Boned)—Med.-Rare	7–9 lbs.	Low/lid closed/direct	15 min. per lb.
	7–9 lbs.	Low/lid closed/indirect (rotisserie)	15 min. per lb.
Lamb Chops	½" thick	Low/lid closed/direct	10 min. (5 min. per side)
	Med.-Rare—1½" thick	Low/lid closed/direct	16 min. (8 min. per side)
	Well Done—1½" thick	Low/lid closed/direct	18 min. (9 min. per side)
Lamb Chops—Stuffed	1½" thick	Low/lid closed/indirect (spit-basket)	12 min. (6 min. per side)
Lamb Shish Kebabs	1¼" cubes	Low/lid closed/direct	12 min. (6 min. per side)
PORK			
Ribs			
Back ribs	4–6 lbs.	Low/lid closed/direct (1 burner)	3 hrs.
Country Ribs	4–6 lbs.	Low/lid closed/direct (1 burner)	3 hrs.
Spareribs	4–6 lbs.	Low/lid closed/direct (1 burner)	2 hrs.
Pork Chops	1" thick	Low/lid closed/direct	25 min. (turn often)
Pork Chops, Smoked	¾" thick	High/lid closed/direct	4 min. (2 min. per side)
Rolled Pork Roast (boneless)	3–4 lbs.	Low/lid closed/indirect (rotisserie)	70 min. per lb.
Pork Loin Roast (boneless)	4–5 lbs.	Low/lid closed/direct	40 min. per lb.
Ham			
Bone in	6½–7 lbs.	Low/lid closed/indirect (rotisserie)	6–6½ min. per lb.
Boneless	3–5 lbs.	Low/lid closed/indirect (rotisserie or roasting rack)	17 min. per lb.
VEAL			
Cutlets	⅛–¼" thick	Low/lid closed/direct	9 min. (4–5 min. per side)
Patties	¾" thick	Med./lid closed/direct	14 min. (7 min. per side)
POULTRY			
Chicken			
Broiler/fryer halves	1 lb. each	Low/lid closed/direct	35 min. (turning)

Meat	Size or Weight	Heat Control	Time
Broiler/fryer	halved	Low/lid closed/indirect (in basket)	30–35 min.
Roasting	5 lbs.	Low/lid closed/indirect (rotisserie)	1¼ hrs.
Roasting—Stuffed	3½ lbs.	Low/lid closed/indirect (rotisserie)	20 min. per lb.
Pieces		Low/lid closed/indirect (warming shelf)	30 min.
Rock Cornish Hens		Low/lid closed/indirect (warming shelf)	50–55 min.
		Low/lid closed/indirect (rotisserie)	50 min.
Capon, Whole	3½ lbs.	Low/lid closed/indirect (roasting rack)	1¼ hrs. (20 min. per lb.)
Turkey			
Whole, small	8–10 lbs.	Low/lid closed/indirect (rotisserie)	6 min. per lb.
Whole, med.–large	12–20 lbs.	Low/lid closed/indirect (roasting rack)	9½ min. per lb.
Stuffed	12–20 lbs.	Low/lid closed/indirect (roasting rack)	11½ min. per lb.
Ground Chicken or Turkey Patties	½" thick	Low/lid closed/direct	14 min. (7 min. per side)
SEAFOOD			
Fish steaks	¼" thick	Low/lid closed/direct	8 min.
Fish fillets	1" thick	Low/lid closed/direct	6 min. (turning)
Pan fish (in foil)	9 oz. each	Low/lid closed/indirect	15 min.
Halibut steaks	¼" thick	Low/lid closed/indirect (two burners, in basket)	15 min.
	1½" thick	Low/lid closed/direct (one burner)	15 min.
Lobster	8 oz. each	Low/lid closed/direct	9 min. (turning)
Rainbow Trout (in foil)	13 oz. each	Low/lid closed/indirect	12 min.
Rainbow Trout, Stuffed	13 oz. each	Low/lid closed/indirect	8 min. (4 min. per side)
Red Snapper Fillets (aluminum foil pan)		Low/lid closed/indirect	6 min.
Salmon Patties	½" thick	Low/lid closed/direct	10 min. (5 min. per side)
Salmon Steaks	½–1" thick	Low/lid closed/direct	10 min. (5 min. per side)
Scampi	jumbo	Low/lid closed/indirect (one burner)	5 min.
Shrimp, on skewers	large	Low/lid closed/direct	8 min. (turning)
Swordfish			
Fillets		Low/lid closed/direct	8 min. (4 min. per side)
Steaks		Low/lid closed/indirect (in basket)	15 min.

8 The Complete Barbecue Cookbook

According to the manufacturers, shiny or dull sides of aluminum foil work in the same way. You can shield or make packages with either side out. In the manufacturing process two pieces of aluminum foil are rolled out together. The side that touches the rollers becomes shiny; the other side, not in direct contact with the rollers, has a matte finish.

(Right) *DRIP PAN OR BAKING SHEET* (1). Use 2 sheets of heavy duty foil 6 inches longer than the desired length of pan. Fold in all edges 1-1/2 to 2 inches. (2). Score corners. (3). Fold again forming 1-1/2 to 2-inch sides and miter corners against sides of pan. For drip pan, place between coals in fire bowl. Let fat cool before removing from grill. For baking sheet, place on grill rack over coals.

Wok Cooking

Included in this book is an entire chapter on wok cooking (see Chapter 9). This new dimension in cooking will add great versatility to your gas grill. Wok cooking is another form of direct-heat cooking. The grid is removed and the wok is placed directly over the briquets, giving the wok a very intense direct heat for stir-frying. Wok cooking on your grill will allow you to stir-fry with the same intense heat used in Oriental restaurants. It will allow you to cook larger amounts of food in your wok more quickly, while giving your food that authentic stir-fry taste.

Cooking with Foil

Heavy-duty aluminum foil and aluminum foil pans are most convenient barbecue accessories. They can be used as cooking containers, drip pans, and/or heat deflectors. Vegetables, such as corn ears and potatoes, are excellent when wrapped in foil. When tightly wrapped, foil-covered foods hold in natural juices, making cooked foods moist and tender. Foil packets allow foods that require seasonings and sauces to be cooked right on the grill. For a smoked or natural barbecue flavor, leave the foil packet loosely wrapped or open at the top to let in smoke.

If you do not have the proper size foil pan, several layers of heavy-duty aluminum foil can be folded and shaped into the proper size to be used as a drip pan to set under roasts or large pieces of meat during grill cooking. These pans catch the juices and prevent charring and/or burning from cooking flare-ups.

Delicate foods such as fish fillets and small whole fish may be cooked on heavy-duty aluminum foil placed directly on the grill. Virtually all sandwich and bread recipes require foil for grilling and/or heating.

Foil also may be used to cover foods after cooking to keep them warm. Leftover foods, without an acid sauce (tomato, wine, vinegar,

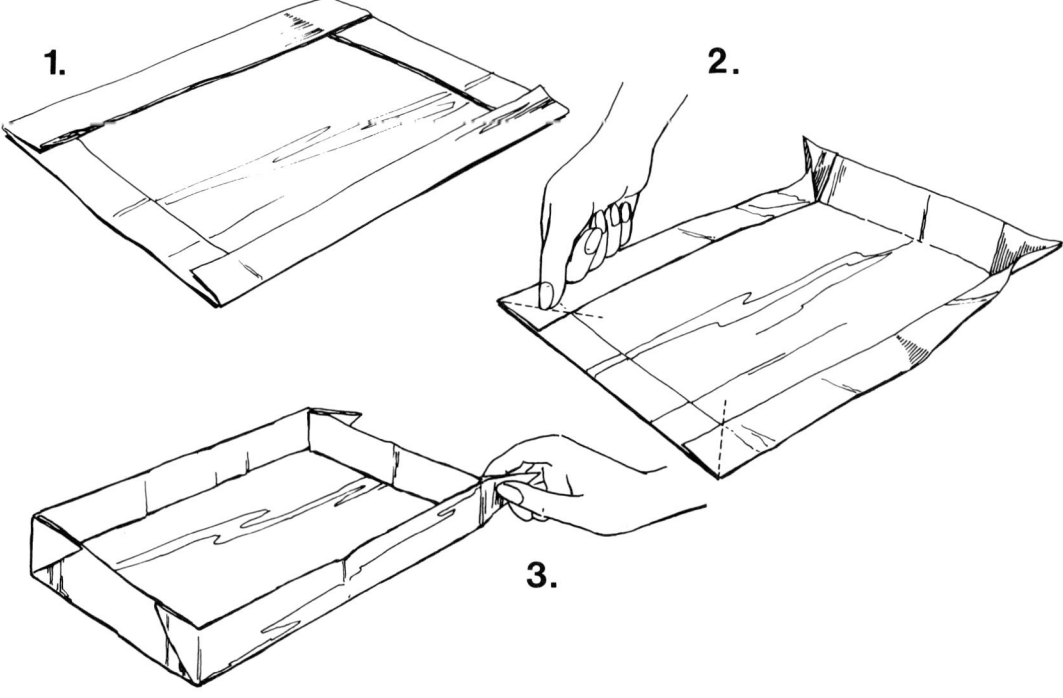

cheese, or lemon juice), may be wrapped in foil for storage. Acid foods will pit the foil.

Foil may be wrapped tightly around foods or formed into an envelope-shaped packet for easy loose food cooking. Always turn foil-wrapped foods with tongs, not a fork, to avoid puncturing the wrap. Many foods may be served right in the foil. Use nonstick vegetable spray on foil to eliminate sticking.

When spit-cooking foods of uneven shape, smaller parts that may cook too fast may be wrapped in foil as a shield against the heat during some of the cooking. Also, a piece of foil may be positioned directly on the briquets to shield a portion of food being cooked directly above.

Preheat unit and turn heat to low. With foil deflector sheet in place, baking dishes and casseroles may be cooked using standard cooking times for a 350° F. oven setting.

Never use foil to line your fire box. Any blockage of air vents or the grease drip hole will alter cooking efficiency and could be dangerous.

Pairing a Microwave with Your Gas Grill

Precook Larger Pieces of Meat in Microwave

Many imaginative cooks who enjoy the flavor of barbecue cooking plus the convenience of microwave units have combined the two with surprisingly good results.

Many meats that require long cooking or defrosting may be started in the microwave and finished on the barbecue. This allows the cook virtually to barbecue right out of the freezer. What used to take overnight or several hours is now accomplished in less than an hour.

Chickens, ribs, and other foods that normally take an hour to barbecue may be cooked by microwave for 10 minutes or so, then cooked over low grill heat for

Because of the many variables such as wind, ambient temperatures, and grill models, always check foil packets every five minutes during the last 10–15 minutes of cooking.

(Left) DRUGSTORE WRAP (1). Place food in center of a sheet of heavy duty foil large enough to permit adequate wrapping. (2). Bring 2 sides of foil up over food. For cooking, fold down loosely in a series of locked folds allowing for heat circulation and expansion. For freezing, fold down in a series of locked folds until foil is tight against food. (3). Fold short ends up and over again; crimp to seal.

Run balancing test on all rotisserie meats before placing on grill.

Test to see if your meat is properly balanced on your spit.

another 10 minutes for glazing or to crisp the outside and impart a barbecue flavor.

Barbecue for Meals Ahead

Foods may be partially cooked on the barbecue and frozen, to be finished later in the microwave. This is especially satisfactory with thick hamburger patties. They should be grilled to very rare at high (just to seal the surfaces), cooled, and frozen. When reheated in the microwave, they retain that fresh-barbecued look and flavor.

Rotisserie Cooking

The advantages of cooking with a rotisserie are many. It does not require constant watching, as the meat is turning continuously; hence the chances of any burning or charring are greatly diminished. The meat is constantly basted in its own juices and basting sauces, which roll around the outside of the meat as the spit turns. The meat stays very moist and flavorful because of this. Slower grilling via a rotisserie also allows excessive fat in your meat to cook out.

Grilling Method

Rotisserie cooking should be done over an aluminum foil drip pan to catch all the meat drippings. These drippings can be used for gravies and sauces, and are quite flavorful. It is best to keep some water in drip pans at all times to prevent flare-ups and burning.

Drip Pans

You can either use an aluminum pan of the proper size or make one with heavy-duty aluminum foil. The drip pan should be no larger in width than the meat on the rotisserie, just large enough to catch all the drippings. Anything larger than that tends to interfere with the heat circulation in your barbecue grill. For larger roasts and turkey the shallow aluminum foil pans are best. It is difficult to hand-fashion a shallow drip pan that doesn't leak, tip, or overflow at one corner. Remember to keep water in the drip pans, refilling them as the water cooks out.

Arranging Meat on Your Spit

Careful attention needs to be paid to the placement of the meat on the spit. The easiest meats to balance on your rotisserie are boneless roasts of uniform shape and texture, such as rolled roasts. Insert one of the holding forks on your spit, then put your spit through the center of the meat. Add the other holding fork and secure tightly in the center of the spit. Irregular roasts are harder to balance, but running the spit through the meat diagonally will help.

Problems Caused by Uneven Balancing

After the holding forks are tightened on your meat, hold the spit loosely in the palms of your hands with the meat in the center. Roll the spit back and forth in the palms of your hands. If it rolls smoothly, the meat will be balanced. If it does not roll smoothly, try to reposition the meat on the spit for better balance. Not only is it a strain on your motor to have the meat on your spit or rotisserie balanced unevenly; it may also cause jerking and uneven turning or fast and slow rolls, which will cause the meat to cook unevenly and possibly burn on the heavier side, while the lighter side will not be as brown or as well done.

How to Cook with Your Gas Grill

Poultry Rotisserie

You may wish to fill the cavity of poultry with onion, garlic, parsley, or celery for flavoring; apples and dried fruit are good additions for game birds, duck, and goose. Poultry should be trussed firmly so that wings, drumsticks, and neck skin are close to the body. Use kitchen twine for trussing. After the bird is on the spit, run the balance test above.

Rotisserie cooking need not be limited to roasts and/or poultry. Such items as ribs can also be skewered back and forth on the spit.

Rotisserie Basket

A rotisserie basket is an invaluable accessory that will aid you in grilling small items such as poultry parts, chops, sausages, hors d'oeuvres, small fish, fish fillets, and fruits.

Meat Thermometer

The most accurate way of telling when your spit-barbecued meat is done is to use a meat thermometer. Place the meat thermometer carefully so that it does not hit the outside, top, or back of your grill. Insert the tip of the thermometer into the thickest part of the meat, taking special care not to let it touch the spit or the bone.

Rotisserie Motor

The rotisserie motor should be removed from the grill when not in use. Leaving it out in the elements for any length of time may cause rusting and deterioration.

TROUBLESHOOTING: SETTING UP AND MAINTAINING YOUR GRILL

Cooking Temperatures

Every Charmglow grill is checked and adjusted at the factory. However, a second adjustment by the owner is advisable when assembling the unit and at least once a year thereafter.

Very little can go wrong with your Charmglow if set up correctly, cleaned, and maintained as described in your owner's guide. Some yellow at the tip of the flame is normal. If the flame is all yellow, adjust as follows. When turning off your grill to a low level, a pop sound is normal. If your grill makes a very loud pop when you turn it off, correct by adjusting the flame as described in your owner's guide.

1. If the grill is hot, turn the gas off and wait for the grill to cool.

2. Remove the parts needed to get at the air shutter (shroud on large housing models, control box cover on smaller housing models).

3. Light your grill. Adjust the air shutter so that the flame is correct. The shutter should be about ½ open on L.P. gas units, ¾ open on natural gas units. Each grill is slightly different; these settings are average.

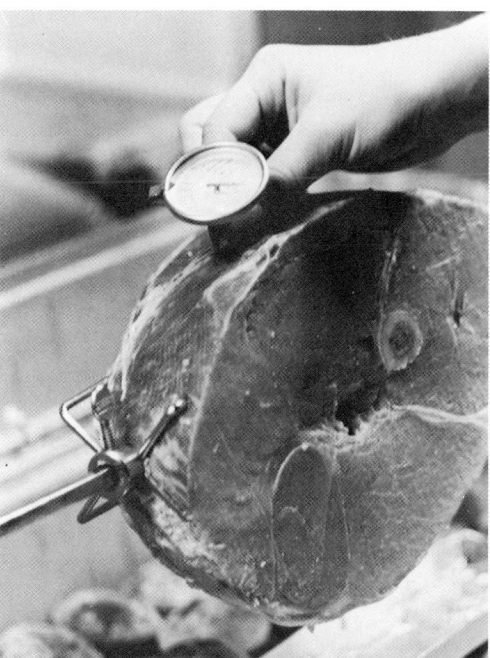

Never light grill with lid closed. Always raise grill lid before lighting.

(Left) Be sure to use a meat thermometer when cooking large pieces of meat or poultry. Cooking times may vary due to wind conditions and position of lid.

Flare-Up

Some flare-ups can be expected with high-fat foods. While this adds a smoky flavor, too much flare-up will cause excessive burning or charring. Use an aluminum foil drip pan for rotisserie foods and watch fatty grilled foods during cooking.

Heat Variations

No two gas barbecue units perform exactly alike, because location, wind, and weather will influence cooking temperatures. A slight breeze across the grill will cool the cooking temperatures by 25–50 degrees. Unit should be turned so that the wind is at the back of the grill, allowing the lid to shield the cooking area.

Experience will show that some grills will heat slightly more at the center and back of the grill surface. Thicker meats or the thickest portion of the food should be positioned at these spots for even cooking.

BENEFITS OF GAS GRILLING

Briefly, here are 10 good reasons why it's great to own a Charmglow barbecue gas grill.

1. The Charmglow gas barbecue is an alternative cooking appliance. This means that when you cook on it you are not using an indoor cooking appliance. Energy is not wasted with the Charmglow; it is simply used in a different way to accomplish the same purpose.

2. You get great outdoor barbecue flavor without charcoal mess. There is no leftover charcoal to burn out, which results in energy waste.

3. The gas barbecue grill will consume considerably less energy than an electric range and about the same amount as a gas range in preparing a given meal.

4. There is no pilot light on a Charmglow. When you turn it to the off position it is 100 percent off. No pilot light means no wasted energy. No energy is needed to start it with lighter fluid or electric elements, as are used with charcoal.

5. When you cook outside you do not fill your house with heat or cooking fumes. This means you do not have to utilize air conditioners or fans to keep the house cool in the summer and/or odor-free.

6. Entertaining your guests at home by preparing a Charmglow meal is not only gracious and fun; it really saves energy. If you take them to a restaurant for dinner, you will spend more money and use more energy just getting there in your car than you would use to prepare the entire meal on your Charmglow grill.

7. Whole-meal cooking is not only possible but common on the gas barbecue, whereas most meals cooked on a range utilize one or more burners, plus oven and/or broiler.

8. The cleanup of the gas barbecue consists mostly of a quick brushing of the cooking grids. Contrast that to the great quantities of hot water needed to clean and rinse all the pots and pans used when the meal is prepared indoors.

9. When you turn your gas off, your unit will cool down quickly. No energy is wasted burning leftover hot coals. Also, you don't have to clean out old coals from your Charmglow gas grill.

10. No matter what happens to other cooking appliances, you will always have a versatile cooking appliance ready for you. Your gas grill can do anything from brewing

---

For safety sake, always turn gas tank off at tank valve when you are through with grill.

Excess fat should be trimmed from meat before grilling to avoid flare-up problems.

Low-Calorie Cooking

While this book is not intended as a guide to the newest low-calorie diet fad, there are several valuable things to remember if watching the waistline is your thing.

First, barbecue cooking can be done with no added fats or oils. No-calorie nonstick cooking sprays work fine on the barbecue grill or on foil packets for barbecue cooking. Marinades and cooking sauces may be made oil-free to flavor meats, poultry, and seafood.

Salt or sugar substitutes may also be used, though sugar-free mixtures will flavor but not glaze. Most calories contained in wine and/or alcohol cook away, leaving only natural flavors.

A great number of calories can be saved through careful selection of meats. Cuts should be as fat-free as possible and trimmed carefully. Skinless chicken breasts are relatively low in calories, as are most types of fish and seafood.

Oriental cooking is also noted for its low calories. Wok cooking on your grill will give you great versatility and variety in low-calorie cooking.

With a little meal planning, dieters can join right in with the rest of the gang at barbecue time.

Gas Pays Off Again and Again

A gas grill pays off from the moment it's fired up. To cook an average-sized chicken on a charcoal grill, the cost in charcoal and lighter fluid is about 80¢. To cook the same size chicken on a modern gas grill, the cost is about 2¢.

The chart below shows the results of extensive tests, which were conducted recently by an independent testing organization.

Backyard chefs have never been so particular, and that's where gas pays off again. Gas cooks foods quickly and allows selective temperature control. A good gas grill can be trusted with the finest

Gas Pays Off

Cooking Method	A Meal of Chicken (Average weight, 2 lbs. 3 oz.)			A Meal of Hamburger (Average weight, ¼ lb.)		
	Average Time (min.)	Average Cost	Average BTUs*	Average Time (min.)	Average Cost	Average BTUs*
Gas grill	52.5	$0.02	9,592	18.5	$0.01	6,035
Electric grill	78	0.12	26,625	42	0.08	18,256
Charcoal grill	72	0.80	85,976	34	0.49	60,026
Gas range	38	0.02	8,874	7	0.01	2,566
Gas convection range	26	0.01	6,365	7.7	0.01	3,699
Electric range	43	0.12	26,544	10.7	0.04	8,052

*Based on primary energy used.

cuts of meat and delivers that unique, smoky, outdoor flavor that results when heated meat juices drip on hot briquets.

Because of gas, backyard grilling has never been easier, and that's worth a lot. It means there's no more fumbling with messy briquets and dangerous lighter fluids. A gas grill is ready to light at the turn of a valve and ready to cook on in no time at all. Then, when the cooking's done, a gas grill even cleans itself up. There's nothing easier.

Gas saves on energy. A quality gas grill is easy to light, cooks food quickly, allows precise heat control, and provides a true smoky-broiled flavor. It can do it all at a fraction of the time, trouble, and energy cost of cooking with charcoal. You might even find that with a new gas grill, since you can "save on the heat," you can spend more on the meat!

Marinades and Sauces

2

For added flavor give your meat a dry rub. Try a tablespoon of rosemary on beef; mint, garlic, and lemon peel on lamb; caraway or crushed juniper berries on pork; and a combination of basil, thyme, and oregano on poultry.

THE SECRET'S IN THE SAUCE

Mastering the secrets of saucing is what gives class to barbecue cooking. Knowing how to flavor, color, tenderize and glaze foods delicately is what sets apart the backyard weekend cook from the classic barbecue chef.

Sauces for barbecue cooking fall into three basic categories: marinades, precooking seasonings, and tenderizers; cooking and basting sauces; and table sauces. Many sauce recipes may be used in two or all three functions.

Sauces and other barbecue seasonings, such as dry rubs, serve a number of important purposes in barbecuing. Here are the most important facts to remember in selecting foods and matching sauces.

FLAVOR

A rich and distinctive flavor is what makes barbecue cooking so different from standard kitchen cooking. Sauces add needed flavors to normally bland meats, poultry, and seafood. Whether a hearty spiced tomato sauce or a delicate wine and herb combination, a sauce combines with the character of smoke and searing heat to create a rewarding and individualistic result. Using a variety of sauces and seasoning recipes with different foods can offer the imaginative barbecue cook unlimited variety and flavor combinations.

It should be remembered that these are basic recipes and may be changed to suit individual tastes. For example, if oregano is listed, and you prefer thyme or rosemary, make the substitution. If wine is not to your liking, substitute fruit juice or bouillon or beer.

No two people have the same taste in foods or seasonings, though many basic tastes are more popular than others. These recipes consist of tested basics and are offered as a start toward imaginative barbecue flavoring.

TENDERNESS

Ideally, only tender cuts of meat should be used for barbecuing. Less tender cuts must be marinated before grilling. Chicken, turkey, and seafoods are generally tender. If a marinade is suggested for these, it will be for flavor only.

Tougher meats, such as pot roast and round steak, are tenderized through enzyme action—the natural breakdown of tough fibers by acids and other factors in wine, vinegar, citrus juices, tomato juice, and tenderizing preparations. Many tenderizing marinades also impart pleasing flavors and are used as cooking sauces as well. Large roasts or tougher meats may require overnight marination, while smaller cuts require only a half-hour or more in the marinade.

Experience will show just how long to marinate each cut of meat (times may change for varying sizes), and the recipes should be used as a guideline only. Care should be taken not to overmarinate with commercial tenderizers (papaya enzyme products), as flavor and texture can be altered too much. Regardless of the tenderizer or marinade, slow cooking is the best way to ensure juicy and tender results with most meats that need to be tenderized.

In some cases pounding thin meats with a tenderizer mallet may be preferable to using a commercial tenderizer.

JUICINESS

Tender barbecue meats are juicy. Marinades and cooking sauces used in barbecue cooking ensure adequate moisture during cooking. Oil-based sauces help seal the surfaces of foods quickly and ensure that a minimum of internal juices is lost.

Olive oil is the best of all oils for barbecue cooking. It is thicker and seals more quickly than standard vegetable oil. Olive oil also lends a continental flavor to marinades and basting sauces that many people enjoy. For economy and/or milder flavor, a mixture of one part olive oil to two parts vegetable oil will suffice.

Wine, fruit or vegetable juice, seasoned broths, and water add moisture to foods while cooking. In combination with oil and seasonings, this moisture is very important in keeping slow-roasted meats moist. For rotisserie cooking an aluminum drip pan is valuable to help retain natural fats and juices, which may be blended with the cooking sauce for added flavor and moisture.

Season meats with herbs and spices—e.g., pepper, cloves for ham—before cooking. *Do not salt.* Salt will draw the natural juices out of your meat, making it drier. If necessary, salt meat just before serving.

If a drip pan is used, skim off excess fat and use any remaining natural juices as a table sauce. The juices can also be cooked together with leftover flavoring marinades or basting sauces. Tenderizing marinades with enzymes should not be used.

GLAZING

Cooking sauces often are designed to glaze or color the surface of foods as well as flavor them. Many cooking sauces contain sugar or honey, which caramelizes when heated, making an attractive barbecue glaze for lamb, pork, and poultry. Sauces that have a tomato base coat foods with the familiar barbecue sauce look and taste. This glazing and coating is generally best when done only during the final 10-15 minutes of cooking, as both sugar and tomato will easily turn black if left over the heat too long. This is the most common cause of barbecue failure when coupled with excessive heat.

Fruit juices, such as orange juice or concentrate, maraschino cherry juice, pineapple juice, and apricot nectar add both flavor and color as glaze ingredients. Fruit preserves and jam, straight out of the jar, may be spread on many barbecue meats during final cooking minutes. Honey and thick fruit liqueurs may also be used.

TABLE SEASONING

Many cooking sauces may be heated and served as a table sauce. These are especially good when mixed with natural cooking juices that are collected in a foil drip pan. Juices, sauce, or both combined may also be thickened as gravy. A splash of wine may be added to enhance the heated sauce or gravy.

Cold table sauces, seasoned butters, and relishes fill out the spectrum of barbecue seasonings. These can all be prepared ahead and served in great variety. Commercial barbecue sauces and table relishes may be "fancied up" with a touch of your own involving spices, wines, fresh minced onions, parsley, etc.

SEASONING THE BRIQUETS

In days past, unique barbecue cooking was the result of selected woods and charcoal to flavor the food. Fruit wood, hickory, mesquite and other aromatic fuels added a distinct flavor during cooking, and this was a trademark of regional American barbecue style.

These flavors may be enjoyed in Charmglow's gas-fired barbecue cooking as well.

Most barbecue cooks have used hickory chips and pieces to embellish charcoal brazier cooking. Hickory, fruit wood, or other aromatic wood chips should be soaked in water at least several hours or overnight. Wrap wet wood chips in heavy-duty foil in a cylinderlike shape, leaving the ends open. Place these foil packets directly on the briquets toward the front or coolest part of the grill. The foil wrap around the wood keeps it from bursting into flame and allows it to smoke the way you want it to. Should the wood chips burst into flame, you can extinguish them with a water mister or baster. Be careful to use only a very small amount of water, just enough to put out the fire.

OTHER SEASONINGS

Rolled and tied roasts may be seasoned in a variety of ways before tying, using prepared seasonings, celery leaves, onion or garlic pieces.

Slivers of garlic, onion, or pepper may be inserted into small slits cut into roasts. Slices of bacon tied around lean meat and seafood lend both flavor and a natural oil baste during cooking.

Marinades and Sauces

CHARMGLOW MARINADE FOR STEAKS

Yield: 1¼ cups

This marinade tenderizes as well as flavors steaks such as round steak.

- 2 tablespoons oil
- ½ cup soy sauce
- 2 tablespoons Worcestershire sauce
- 1 tablespoon dry mustard
- ¼ teaspoon finely ground pepper
- ¼ cup wine vinegar
- 1 teaspoon chopped fresh parsley
- 2 cloves garlic, crushed (optional)
- ¼ cup lemon juice

Combine all ingredients and mix well. Store in the refrigerator until ready to use.

CHARMGLOW BAR-B-Q SAUCE

Yield: about 2 cups

This is a good basic barbecue sauce that is great on all types of ribs, pork roast, chops, and poultry. It will keep in the refrigerator for several weeks.

- 1 cup ketchup
- ¼ cup vinegar
- 1 tablespoon dry mustard
- 1 tablespoon dark brown sugar
- 1 teaspoon paprika
- 1 teaspoon pepper
- ¼ teaspoon red pepper
- 1 drop Tabasco sauce
- 1 teaspoon salt
- 1 tablespoon butter
- Juice and peel of ½ lemon
- 1 clove garlic, crushed
- 1 sprig parsley, chopped
- 1 stalk celery, minced

Mix together all ingredients or combine them in a blender or food processor. Then transfer to a saucepan and cook over medium heat until the sauce simmers. Continue cooking on low for 5 minutes so that all the flavors are blended.

BARBECUE SAUCE FOR ORIENTAL SPARERIBS

Yield: 1½ cups (enough for 4-6 pounds of ribs)

This sauce gives a nice tangy flavor.

- ¼ cup soy sauce
- ⅔ cup wine vinegar
- ½ cup pineapple juice
- 1 teaspoon fresh ginger root, grated, or ½ teaspoon ground ginger

Combine ingredients and brush ribs generously and frequently while grilling (see instructions for Oriental Barbecued Ribs).

(Below) Spit-barbecued roasts which require basting should always be cooked using a foil drip pan. Basting should begin during the last one-third or half hour of cooking. Care should be taken with tomato-base sauces as they do burn after 15 minutes cooking.

Marinades and basting sauces are suggested as a starting point in barbecue cooking. Recipes may be changed by switching herbs, wines, oils, and application methods to appeal to individual tastes. It is wise to try a tested recipe as originally suggested before altering it. Then you will know whether it has been improved.

BASIC POULTRY MARINADE

Yield: 1 cup

This has a very pleasing taste and can be used on all domestic poultry and pheasants. It's probably a bit too mild for wild duck and geese.

½ cup olive oil or cooking oil
⅓ cup dry white wine
¼ cup white wine vinegar
1 clove garlic, crushed
1 teaspoon dry mustard
½ teaspoon poultry seasoning
½ teaspoon celery salt
1 teaspoon salt
¼ teaspoon pepper

Shake ingredients together in a jar. Pour over poultry. Let stand 4 hours or overnight, turning several times. During cooking, brush each piece with marinade when turning, or every 20 minutes for poultry on a spit or in a spit basket.

SOY SAUCE FOR BARBECUED FISH

Yield: about 1½ cups

A very interesting fish marinade, recommended for fish such as haddock and scrod.

4 tablespoons butter
1 clove garlic, crushed
½ cup ketchup
¼ cup dry red wine
1 tablespoon lemon juice
1 teaspoon Worcestershire sauce
2 tablespoons prepared mustard
¼ teaspoon pepper
½ cup soy sauce

Place all ingredients except soy sauce in a small saucepan. Cook over low heat, stirring often. When butter has melted, remove from heat and add soy sauce. Pour over fish or baste during cooking.

PORK BASTING SAUCE

Yield: 1½ cups

Good on any type of pork.

½ cup brown sugar
4 tablespoons honey
1 cup orange, pineapple, or grapefruit juice
¼ teaspoon dry mustard

Combine all ingredients in a small saucepan and heat over moderate heat (or in a microwave oven) until the sugar is completely dissolved. Use only during the last 20-25 minutes of cooking for a roast or other large piece of meat. For pork chops, add sauce during the last 10 minutes of grilling and watch carefully. This basting sauce has sugar in it, which burns easily.

ROQUEFORT SAUCE FOR STEAK

Yield: about ⅓ cup

For that gourmet touch!

1 teaspoon Worcestershire sauce
2 ounces Roquefort cheese
¼ cup sour cream
¼ teaspoon pepper
Salt to taste
Green onions or chives

Combine all the ingredients in a small bowl. Spread cheese sauce on steak just before serving to let it melt.

WILD GAME MARINADE

Yield: 1¾ cups

This marinade tenderizes your meat—venison, rabbit, or game birds—and enhances its flavor.

- 1 cup cooking oil
- ½ cup dry red wine
- 2 tablespoons minced onion
- 1 clove garlic, minced
- 1 tablespoon mashed juniper berries or ¼ teaspoon allspice or cloves
- ½ teaspoon pepper
- 1 bay leaf
- ½ teaspoon thyme
- 1 teaspoon salt

Shake ingredients together in a jar or mix in a blender. Marinate game in the refrigerator for 1 or 2 days, depending on size and toughness. Turn game twice a day. Use the remaining marinade to baste the game during cooking.

SWEET AND SOUR BASTING SAUCE

Yield: about 2⅓ cups

Particularly good with pork and poultry.

- ¼ cup cooking oil
- ⅔ cup wine vinegar
- ½ cup pineapple juice
- ¼ cup soy sauce
- ⅔ cup brown sugar
- 1 teaspoon ginger root, grated, or ½ teaspoon dry ground ginger

Combine ingredients in a small saucepan. Cook until sugar is completely dissolved.

GINGER BASTING SAUCE

Yield: about 1 cup

Delicious on chicken and pork and meat such as flank and chuck steaks.

- 1 tablespoon brown sugar
- ½ tablespoon cornstarch
- 2 tablespoons fresh ginger root, grated, or ½ teaspoon powdered ginger
- 2 cloves garlic, crushed
- ¼ cup wine vinegar
- ⅓ cup soy sauce
- ⅓ cup apricot jam

Stir ingredients together until sugar is dissolved. Let stand for 1 hour to blend flavors. Heat mixture until thickened and stir well before brushing on pork or poultry during final 10 minutes of cooking.

TOMATO SAUCE

Yield: about 1¼ cups

Use this easy-to-make sauce for delicious Italian Sausage sandwiches (see recipe for Italian Sausage).

- 1 green pepper, cut into julienne strips
- 1 tablespoon butter or margarine
- 1 8-ounce can tomato sauce
- 1 tablespoon grated Parmesan cheese
- ¼ teaspoon garlic powder
- ½ teaspoon oregano

Sauté green pepper strips in butter or margarine. Place remaining ingredients in a separate saucepan and heat through. Pour sauce over Italian sausage on rolls and top with sautéed green peppers.

A simple way of marinating large pieces of meat is to put meat into a plastic bag and pour marinade over meat. Put plastic bag and marinade in a snug-fitting container or bowl. Seal bag tightly with twist. Be sure to keep the bag with the tied end up to avoid leakage. Self-locking plastic bags of the proper size may also be used.

Marinades and Sauces

SOY DIPPING SAUCE

Yield: ¾ cup

A nice dipping sauce for shrimp, this one gives an Oriental flavor to poultry and beef as well.

- 1 tablespoon cornstarch
- 3 tablespoons soy sauce
- ¼ cup water
- ¼ cup sake or dry sherry
- 1 tablespoon toasted sesame seed oil (see note below) or melted butter

Dissolve cornstarch in soy sauce in a small saucepan. Add water and wine and heat to boiling, stirring constantly. Remove from heat when mixture is clear and thick. Add sesame oil or butter. Serve warm.

Note: Toasted sesame oil is available in Oriental markets and specialty shops. It is usually imported from Japan and is not to be confused with the clear sesame oil used for cooking in the Middle East.

CHINESE HOT MUSTARD SAUCE

Yield: ¼ cup

Use as a dipping sauce for any Oriental dish or appetizer.

- 2 tablespoons dry mustard
- 2 tablespoons hot water
- 1 tablespoon dijon mustard

In a small sauce dish, combine dry mustard with hot water, stirring until well blended and smooth. Add prepared mustard, stirring until well blended. Let set at room temperature about 15 minutes to develop full flavor. A little bit of this sauce goes a long way. The addition of the prepared mustard gives the sauce a creamy texture.

SEAFOOD COCKTAIL SAUCE

Yield: ⅓ cup

This sauce is especially good with shrimp served as a first course.

- 1 tablespoon lemon juice
- 2 tablespoons ketchup
- 1 tablespoon chili sauce
- 1 tablespoon hot barbecue sauce (see note below)
- Tabasco sauce to taste (optional) (see note below)
- 1 teaspoon Worcestershire sauce
- ¼ teaspoon garlic salt

Mix all ingredients well. Serve separately or pour over the shrimp. Lemon wedges may also be served.

Note: For a hotter sauce, use 3 teaspoons of barbecue sauce or use regular barbecue sauce and add Tabasco to taste.

SWEET AND SOUR DIPPING SAUCE

Yield: 1¼ cups

A nice accompaniment for many Oriental dishes.

- ¼ cup brown sugar
- 1 tablespoon cornstarch
- ¼ cup cider vinegar
- ¾ cup pineapple juice
- 1 tablespoon soy sauce

Combine ingredients in a saucepan. Cook over medium heat, stirring until sauce thickens and becomes clear.

(Far Left) Imaginative ingredients can be used to create delicious dipping sauces.

SWEET AND SOUR TABLE SAUCE

Yield: about 3½ cups

This sauce can also be used as a basting sauce during the end of the grilling time.

- 1 20-ounce can crushed pineapple, drained
- 1¼ cups pineapple juice
- 3 tablespoons cornstarch
- 1 tablespoon soy sauce
- 3 tablespoons wine vinegar
- ⅓ cup water
- ½ cup brown sugar
- 2 green peppers, chopped

Drain pineapple and measure juice. In a saucepan, combine all ingredients except pineapple and peppers. Cook until thickened, stirring constantly. Add pineapple and peppers and cook 5 minutes longer, or until fruit is heated through. Serve with pork, lamb, poultry, and kebabs.

BROWN BUTTER SAUCE

Yield: ½ cup

This marvelous sauce is particularly good over fish and fresh vegetables such as asparagus, broccoli, cabbage, and cauliflower.

- ½ cup butter
- 2 tablespoons lemon juice
- Freshly ground pepper (optional)
- Chopped parsley, chives, or dill (optional)

In a saucepan over moderate heat, let the butter bubble and foam until it becomes lightly browned. (Cooking it too fast, over heat that is too high will burn the butter.) When butter is a nice golden brown, remove it from the heat and add lemon juice, pepper and herbs. This can also be done in a microwave oven by putting the butter into a 1-cup measuring cup and letting it cook and bubble until it turns golden brown, approximately 4–5 minutes.

BÉARNAISE SAUCE

Yield: 1 cup

A heavenly sauce that embellishes any meat or fish.

- 1 tablespoon chopped shallots
- 2 tablespoons dried tarragon
- 2 tablespoons dried chervil
- 1 sprig thyme
- ½ bay leaf
- ¼ cup vinegar
- ¼ cup white wine
- Pinch salt
- Dash pepper
- 2 egg yolks
- 1 tablespoon water
- ¼ pound butter
- Lemon juice
- Dash cayenne

In a saucepan, combine chopped shallots, herbs, vinegar, wine, and salt and pepper. Bring to a boil and boil down to one-third of the original amount. Strain and cool slightly. Add egg yolks mixed with 1 tablespoon of water. Beat into the sauce with a wire whisk and warm over low heat. As soon as the egg yolks begin to thicken, add the butter, one tablespoon at a time, continuously working with the whisk. Taste and season with lemon juice and a dash of cayenne.

Appetizers

3

When eating outdoors, you'll especially love the convenience of a variety of appetizers and hors d'oeuvres you can prepare and serve directly from your grill. There is no need to heat up your kitchen oven, nor will you need to run back and forth to your guests on the patio or deck. In this chapter you will find a fantastic variety of appetizers.

Go through your own recipe file for additional ideas. You'll find more appetizer recipes that can easily be adapted to cooking on your grill. Just remember, any of your favorite appetizers that need to be heated, baked, cooked, broiled or grilled may be prepared on your grill. Using techniques in this book and the following suggestions, you can readily adapt your own favorite family recipes to grill cooking.

ADAPTING YOUR FAVORITE RECIPES FOR BARBECUE COOKING

Dishes that only need to be heated through before serving can be placed in an oven-proof dish or on foil, then placed on the warming shelf. Allow sufficient time for food to heat through. As a rule of thumb, allow more time for foods that are covered with foil or heated in a covered container than those warmed on a cookie sheet or in uncovered foil pans.

Appetizers that require baking are usually best cooked on your gas grill via the indirect cooking method. If there is insufficient room on your warming shelf, you can add a brick or two directly to the grid. Set the baking pan or sheet on the bricks for a moderate baking temperature. High temperature baking for short periods of time can be done easily on a heavy griddle or pan placed directly on the grids.

Cooking can be done in a bake-and-serve dish with direct heat. Set the temperature control on low. Stir at least every five or ten minutes until you get the feel of cooking on your grill.

Recipes that call for broiling or grilling can be placed in a rotisserie basket for effortless grilling. Small appetizers such as escargot and spinach balls are more easily grilled in rotisserie baskets than any other way. You don't have to worry about food falling through the grids, and the job of turning food frequently is also eliminated.

Grilling and broiling of larger foods can easily be done by placing food directly on the grids over hot coals. Hors d'oeuvres with a high fat content (for example, any items wrapped in bacon), are best grilled directly over hot coals at the start, then finished by indirect cooking method.

A fun way to entertain is to serve an entire meal of hors d'oeuvres. Make and serve a large quantity of various appetizers. Choose a variety of recipes—appetizers made with poultry, seafood, vegetables, cheese, and an assortment of meats. It's probably a bit more expensive and a great deal more work, but it's also a lot more fun. Your guests can help with the grilling, heating, or cooking on your grill. Serve them with a variety of breads, rolls, or crackers. A large tossed salad or a platter of marinated vegetables is a nice accompaniment and economical, which will help make the more expensive appetizer items go further.

RUMAKI

Yield: 36 appetizers
Heat Control: low, lid closed, rotisserie basket

This classic appetizer tastes quite different when cooked on the grill instead of broiled in your stove.

36 chicken livers
36 water chestnuts
18 bacon strips, halved
1 cup soy sauce
½ teaspoon ground ginger
½ teaspoon curry powder

Wrap each liver around a water chestnut. Precook the bacon until almost done but *not* crisp. (You may wish to cook it in a microwave oven for about ¾ minute per strip.) Then wrap each piece of bacon around a chicken liver and secure with a toothpick. Combine the remaining ingredients and pour over the assembled rumaki. Marinate at least 1 hour. Place in a rotisserie basket and cook on low, with the lid closed, for 6 minutes.

PORK STRIPS WITH HOT MUSTARD

Yield: approximately 2 dozen skewers
Heat Control: low, lid closed, direct heat

Although these pork strips are good served warm, they are even better served cold the next day. Try them both ways.

2 pounds lean pork
1 clove garlic, crushed
1 teaspoon salt
1 teaspoon paprika
1 tablespoon ketchup
½ cup dry white wine
1 teaspoon soy sauce
1 recipe Chinese Hot Mustard Sauce (see recipe)

Cut the pork into strips (1 by 3 inches and about ¼ inch thick). Place the pork in a bowl. Combine the remaining ingredients and pour over the pork. Marinate in the refrigerator for at least 24 hours. Place the pork strips on wooden or bamboo skewers. Cook on low, with the lid closed, until golden brown and glossy, turning frequently, about 10 minutes. Serve as an appetizer with Chinese Hot Mustard Sauce.

BEEF ROLL-UPS

Yield: approximately 40–48 appetizers or 8 entrée servings
Heat Control: low, lid closed, direct heat

These can be served as an entrée or appetizer.

½ pound bacon
⅔ cup chopped onions
1 cup seasoned breadcrumbs
⅔ cup chopped mushrooms
4 tablespoons chopped parsley
2 teaspoons dried basil
Pepper to taste
8 sandwich steaks
Soy sauce for basting (optional)

Precook the bacon in a skillet or the oven until the bacon is cooked but not crisp (or cook in a microwave oven for 5 minutes). Cut into pieces. Combine bacon, onions, breadcrumbs, mushrooms, parsley, dried basil, and pepper. Spread the crumb mixture on the sandwich steaks, roll up, and secure with toothpicks. Place on the grill over low heat, with the lid closed, for 10 minutes (5 minutes on each side). You may baste each side with soy sauce as you turn them.

A barbecue flavor is obtained with a gas-fired grill when fats and cooking juices hit the hot briquets and create aromatic smoke that surrounds foods being cooked.

SHRIMP 'N' DILL APPETIZER

Yield: approximately 24–32 appetizers

Heat Control: low (1 burner), lid closed, direct heat

This dish may also be served as an entrée for four people.

- 2 pounds fresh jumbo shrimp
- ½ cup sauterne
- ½ teaspoon dried dill
- ½ teaspoon garlic salt
- ½ teaspoon seasoned salt
- ¼ teaspoon hot sauce

Shell and devein the shrimp. Mix the remaining ingredients and toss with the shrimp. Form a large packet of double-thick aluminum foil. Place the ingredients inside and secure tightly. Put the packet directly on the grill and cook on low (1 burner), with the lid closed, for 7 minutes, or until steam escapes from the packet. Serve immediately.

Care should be taken when opening foil-wrapped packets that have been on the grill because of escaping steam.

ANGELS ON HORSEBACK

Yield: 2 dozen appetizers

Heat Control: low, lid closed, direct heat

A New England favorite.

- 12 slices bacon, halved
- 24 large fresh oysters, drained
- ½ teaspoon onion salt
- ¼ teaspoon pepper
- ¼ teaspoon paprika
- 2 tablespoons chopped parsley

Precook the bacon until it is partially cooked but not crisp. Place an oyster on each piece of bacon. Sprinkle with seasonings and parsley. Roll up bacon to enclose oysters and secure with toothpicks. Cook directly on the grill on low, with the lid closed, for 10 minutes, turning often with tongs. When the bacon has browned, serve hot as appetizers.

CHEESE CRISPIES

Yield: 24 wedges

Heat Control: medium (1 burner) and then low (1 burner), lid closed

A marvelous appetizer that you can just keep replenishing as your guests eat them.

- 4 ounces white or yellow sharp cheddar cheese, grated
- 4 ounces Monterey Jack cheese, grated
- 2 12-inch flour tortillas or 3 7-inch flour tortillas
- 2 tablespoons melted butter

Toss the grated cheeses so they are evenly mixed. When using two cheeses of the same color the cheese crispies will have a uniform color; however, when two colors of cheeses are used, the yellow and white, they will have a speckled or confetti look.

Brush the tortillas generously with melted butter on both sides. Place the tortillas on a large cookie sheet or pizza pan over a medium grill and cook for 3 minutes with the lid closed. Tortillas should be crisp and lightly browned. Watch carefully, because they burn easily. Sprinkle the cheese evenly on the toasted tortillas and return to the grill for 2–3 minutes on low, until the cheeses are thoroughly melted.

You may wish to garnish these with little bits of green chilies, taco sauce, guacamole, refried beans, and/or chopped tomatoes or olives, or whatever you prefer. When having a large group, it is a nice idea to set the condiments out and let your guests fix their own. Cut tacos into wedges, pizza style, with shears or a pizza cutter. For variation use all Monterey Jack cheese, sharp cheddar, or sharp longhorn colby.

HAWAIIAN BAMBOO BEEF APPETIZERS

Yield: about 2 dozen
Heat Control: medium, lid closed, direct heat

A fun way to serve your guests appetizers is to have them cook their own to the desired degree of doneness.

¼ teaspoon crushed pepper
¼ cup water
2 cloves garlic, mashed
½ cup chopped onions
½ cup soy sauce
4 tablespoons sugar
1 2-inch piece fresh ginger root, peeled and sliced
4 teaspoons cornstarch
½ cup water
2 pounds beef sirloin, cut into bite-sized pieces
Bamboo skewers

In a saucepan, combine the first 8 ingredients and cook over moderate heat, for about 20 minutes. Blend the cornstarch and water, gradually stir into the sauce, and cook until the mixture is clear and thick. Pour the mixture through a wire strainer, pressing out all the juices, and discard the pulp. Add the beef pieces to the marinade and allow to stand, covered, for about 2 hours. Depending on the size of the meat pieces, thread 3-4 pieces of meat on each skewer and barbecue over medium heat, with the lid closed, for about 4 minutes, turning the skewers once or twice.

STUFFED MUSHROOMS

Yield: between 2-3 dozen, depending on size of mushrooms
Heat Control: low, lid closed, warming shelf

These tasty morsels can be used as appetizers or an accompaniment to beef dishes, such as steak, rolled roast, etc.

¼ pound bacon
1 pound large mushrooms
⅓ cup chopped onions
1 cup seasoned breadcrumbs
2 tablespoons chopped parsley
1 teaspoon dried basil
2 tablespoons olive oil or bacon grease
Pepper to taste
Oil for brushing

Precook the bacon in a skillet or the oven until it is cooked but not crisp (or in microwave oven for 3 minutes). Cut into pieces. Wash the mushrooms and remove the stems and chop. Combine bacon, onions, breadcrumbs, mushroom stems, parsley, dried basil, oil or bacon grease, and pepper. Brush the mushroom caps with oil. Place the mushrooms in an aluminum foil pan and add enough of the breadcrumb mixture to fill each mushroom. Place on the warming shelf and cook on low, with the lid closed, for about 8 minutes, or until the top of the crumb mixture is golden brown in each mushroom.

CHA SHUI (CHINESE PORK APPETIZER)

Yield: approximately 2 dozen appetizers
Heat Control: low, lid closed, direct heat

Although this is really good when it is warm, it tastes even better when refrigerated. You can make two meals at once—make enough for dinner and serve the rest for appetizers at another time.

2	pounds pork tenderloin
1/4	cup soy sauce
1/4	cup brown sugar
2	tablespoons sherry
1	teaspoon onion powder
1	teaspoon cinnamon
2	tablespoons olive oil

Trim the pork of all fat. Combine the remaining ingredients and pour over the meat. Marinate for at least 2 hours. Place on the grill and cook on low, with the lid closed, for 35–45 minutes, or until done. Turn and baste frequently until all sides are brown. Cool and refrigerate. Cut into very thin diagonal slices and serve with Chinese Hot Mustard Sauce, Sweet and Sour Sauce, or Soy Dipping Sauce (see recipes).

CHINESE CHICKEN BREASTS

Yield: about 72 small appetizers or 6 entrée servings
Heat Control: low, lid closed, indirect heat

Serve these as an appetizer or entrée. As an entrée, serve with rice and Fresh Asparagus in Wok (see Index).

6	large whole chicken breasts (skinless and boneless)
1/3	cup dry sherry
1/3	cup Hoisin sauce (see note below)
1/3	cup soy sauce
1/3	cup brown sugar
2	cloves garlic, crushed

Cut the chicken breasts in half and place in a shallow pan. Combine the remaining ingredients and cook until sugar is dissolved. Pour over the chicken and marinate for 3–4 hours in the refrigerator. Grill on low, with the lid closed, for 10 minutes, turning frequently. This method will give the chicken breasts a distinct glaze. When serving as an appetizer cut the chicken into 1-inch pieces and serve with leftover sauce for dipping.

Variation: Place the marinated breasts in a large shallow aluminum foil pan and grill for 15 minutes, turning once and adding sauce as needed.

(Below) As an entree, Cha Shui is best served with rice and stir-fried vegetables.

Note: Hoisin sauce may be purchased in any Oriental store and in many supermarkets in 1-pound jars or cans. It keeps well at room temperature and adds a unique flavor to many dishes.

CHINESE SPARERIBS WITH BLACK-BEAN SAUCE

Yield: 18–24 appetizers

Heat Control: high and then low, lid closed, wok on briquets

Have the butcher cut the spareribs crosswise into 1- or 1½-inch pieces and serve as an appetizer finger food.

- 2 pounds spareribs, cut into 1- or 1½-inch pieces
- Boiling water
- 5 tablespoons fermented black beans
- 3 large cloves garlic
- 4 thin slices fresh ginger root, minced, or ¼ teaspoon ground ginger
- 2 teaspoons sugar
- 2 teaspoons cornstarch
- 3 tablespoons vinegar
- 3 tablespoons chicken broth
- 3 tablespoons soy sauce
- 3 tablespoons dry sherry
- 2 tablespoons salad oil
- 2 green onions, sliced thin
- 1 teaspoon toasted sesame oil

Drop the spareribs into boiling water, heat for 4 minutes, then drain and rinse in cold water (this removes excess fat).

Wash and drain the black beans and crush together with the garlic and ginger root. Combine the sugar, cornstarch, vinegar, chicken broth, soy sauce, and sherry.

Remove grids from the grill. Heat the salad oil in a large, heavy frying pan or wok placed directly over the Charm-Rok on high. When the oil is very hot, add the spareribs and brown them quickly. Add the black bean mixture and stir-fry for a few seconds. Pour the soy sauce mixture over the spareribs and continue stirring. Add the onions, cover, and continue cooking on low with the lid closed, stirring occasionally, until tender, 35–40 minutes. Add sesame oil, stir and serve immediately.

TERIYAKI CHICKEN WINGS

Yield: approximately 40-50 appetizers

Heat Control: low, lid closed, direct heat

This tasty treat is a fine start to any meal.

- 3 pounds chicken wings
- 1 cup soy sauce
- 1 tablespoon brown sugar
- ½ cup melted butter
- ¾ cup water
- 1 tablespoon grated fresh ginger root
- ¼ teaspoon onion powder
- ¼ teaspoon garlic powder

Place the chicken wings in a shallow baking dish. Combine the remaining ingredients in a saucepan and heat until the sugar and butter dissolve. Cool and pour over the chicken. Marinate for 2 hours in the refrigerator. Place the chicken wings directly on the grill and cook over low for 15–20 minutes (depending on the size of the chicken wings), with the lid closed. Turn frequently (basting is not needed).

PINEAPPLE PORK TERIYAKI

Yield: approximately 48 appetizers
Heat Control: low, lid closed, direct heat

This also makes a most attractive entrée served with rice and stir-fried asparagus (see recipe).

- 3½–4 pounds lean boneless pork sirloin
- 1 16-ounce can pineapple chunks (reserve liquid)
- ⅓ cup soy sauce
- 1 teaspoon ground ginger
- 1 large clove garlic, minced or pressed

Cut the pork into 1-inch cubes. Combine the pineapple liquid, soy sauce, ginger, and garlic. Pour over the meat in a shallow dish. Let marinate at least 1 hour. Drain the meat and thread on skewers alternately with pineapple chunks (soak wooden skewers in water for at least 1 hour). Place on the grill and cook on low, with the lid closed, turning and basting frequently, for 20 minutes, or until meat is browned and cooked. This is good served with Sweet and Sour Sauce (see recipe).

Meats

4

Barbecue cooking generally centers around meat. Meat is the "show-off" specialty of most American barbecue meals and deserves special attention.

Barbecue cooking got its start thousands of years ago when primitive man cooked bits of meat on a stick over an open fire. Throughout recorded history open-pit meat cookery has changed very little. Only in the past few decades has barbecue cooking become sophisticated.

But all the fancy sauces and equipment available can't save a poor piece of meat!

The surest way to ensure barbecue success is to select the proper cut of the best possible grade of meat and then prepare it using a reliable and complementary recipe. Only USDA prime and choice grades are recommended.

Equally important is fat. A little fat marbling throughout steaks and roasts is necessary for tenderness and juiciness, but too much fat can cause problems. Always have the butcher trim off excess fat or do so yourself. For very lean meat, such as veal roast, bacon can be wrapped around the roast. A little fat is a must for optimum flavor.

Sauces and marinades tenderize, flavor, and garnish meats. Many variations of the recipes in this book are possible. Your taste and individual experimentation soon will help you develop favorites.

With the exception of steaks and chops, slow cooking generally ensures that meat will be tender. Use low heat for grilled foods, including hamburgers and hot dogs. Roasts and rotisserie recipes can be seared on high in cold weather, or on medium for a few minutes on each side (to seal in the natural juices), and then cooked on low until the proper internal temperature registers on your meat thermometer. A meat thermometer is a must for long-cooking meats as time will vary with weather and location.

FROZEN MEATS

Large roasts and thick steaks should be thawed and brought to room temperature before cooking. Thin steaks, hamburgers, and hot dogs may be started frozen; however, additional cooking time must be allowed.

STEAK COOKING TIPS

Frozen steaks may be thawed in a marinade or oil to help retain juices and to add flavor. *Do not salt steaks before cooking as it will draw out juices, making meat dry.*

Rub steaks with oil or use an oil-based marinade. This helps seal the surface of the steak and holds the juices in. Sear steaks quickly on high or medium, then finish them on low for best results. Always turn steaks with tongs or a spatula, never puncturing with a fork, as this causes loss of valuable juices.

To determine doneness, press steak with a finger. The steak will get firmer as it cooks to well done. Watch juices, which will turn from red for rare, to pink for medium, to broth color for well done. If necessary, make a small cut with a sharp knife alongside the bone or into the thickest part to check thick steaks for doneness.

Serve steaks immediately after cooking. They will lose juices and become tough if held after cooking. A little seasoned butter (see recipes) placed on top of steaks as soon as cooked will add gourmet flavors to any cut.

To achieve the "cross-char" marking used by restaurant grill chefs, give steak a quarter-turn on both sides halfway through cooking to sear in grill marks that cross.

ROAST COOKING TIPS

Use oil or a marinade on roasts to help seal surfaces and hold in juices. Use a foil drip pan when cooking meats with heavy fat content. Always add water to foil drip pans to prevent flare-ups. Outsides may be seared at high or medium, but lengthy cooking should be done on low.

Brush on tomato sauces and glazes (anything with a sugar content) only during the final period of cooking to prevent surface charring. Oil, wine, and broth or juice-based cooking sauces and marinades may be used throughout cooking.

Limit rotisserie roasts to eight to ten pounds to avoid possible contact with briquets. Use a four- or five-pound roast that is long rather than round on small grills. If long rather than round, a roast of eight to ten pounds will cook properly on a large grill. Be sure that all spit-cooked meats are securely tied and fastened to the spit rod.

Allow roasts to sit at least 10–15 minutes after cooking to keep juices from being lost during carving. Grill-cooked roasts may be wrapped in foil to keep them warm.

Whenever possible, reserve drip pan juices or any juices lost during the meat's standing period prior to carving, and add them to flavoring sauces or gravy.

BEEF STEAKS FOR BARBECUING

Steaks should be a minimum of one inch thick, preferably 1½ inches. This allows the chef to sear the steaks on high for 2 minutes on each side to seal in the natural juices and then continue grilling on low until the proper degree of doneness is reached.

Steaks from the loin are the tenderest and most tasty. However, other steaks can be equally good when properly cooked.

Club Steak: One of the smaller loin steaks and ideal for barbecuing. Allow one steak—about one inch thick—per person.

T-Bone Steak: Similar to the club steak and easily recognized by the shape of the bone. Allow about one pound per serving.

Large roasts are best cooked by the indirect heat method.

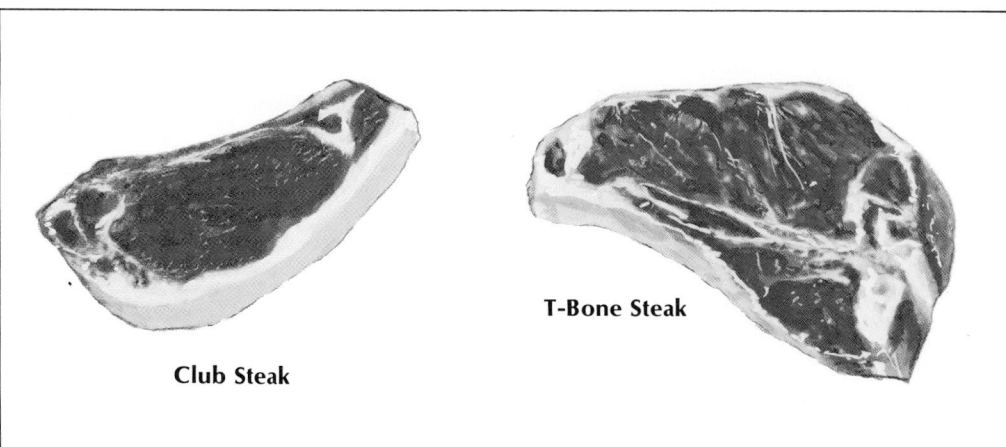

Club Steak

T-Bone Steak

Tenderloin Steak: The smaller muscle steak is known as the tenderloin or as filet mignon. This is the very best. Allow ⅓–½ pound per serving.

Sirloin Steak: The largest of the loin steaks. This cut is great for serving a crowd. Allow ¾ pound per person.

Rib Steak: This is one of the tastiest beef cuts. Each steak is cut from the entire rib section. Allow one steak per person.

Round Steak: This and similar cuts should be marinated and tenderized. Allow ¾ pound per serving.

Sirloin Tip Steak: This is a tender boneless cut that lends itself well to grilling. Order meat 1½ inches thick. Allow ⅓–½ pound per serving.

Butt Steak: Usually a less expensive cut of lean boneless meat that lends itself well to marinating. Allow ⅓–½ pound per serving.

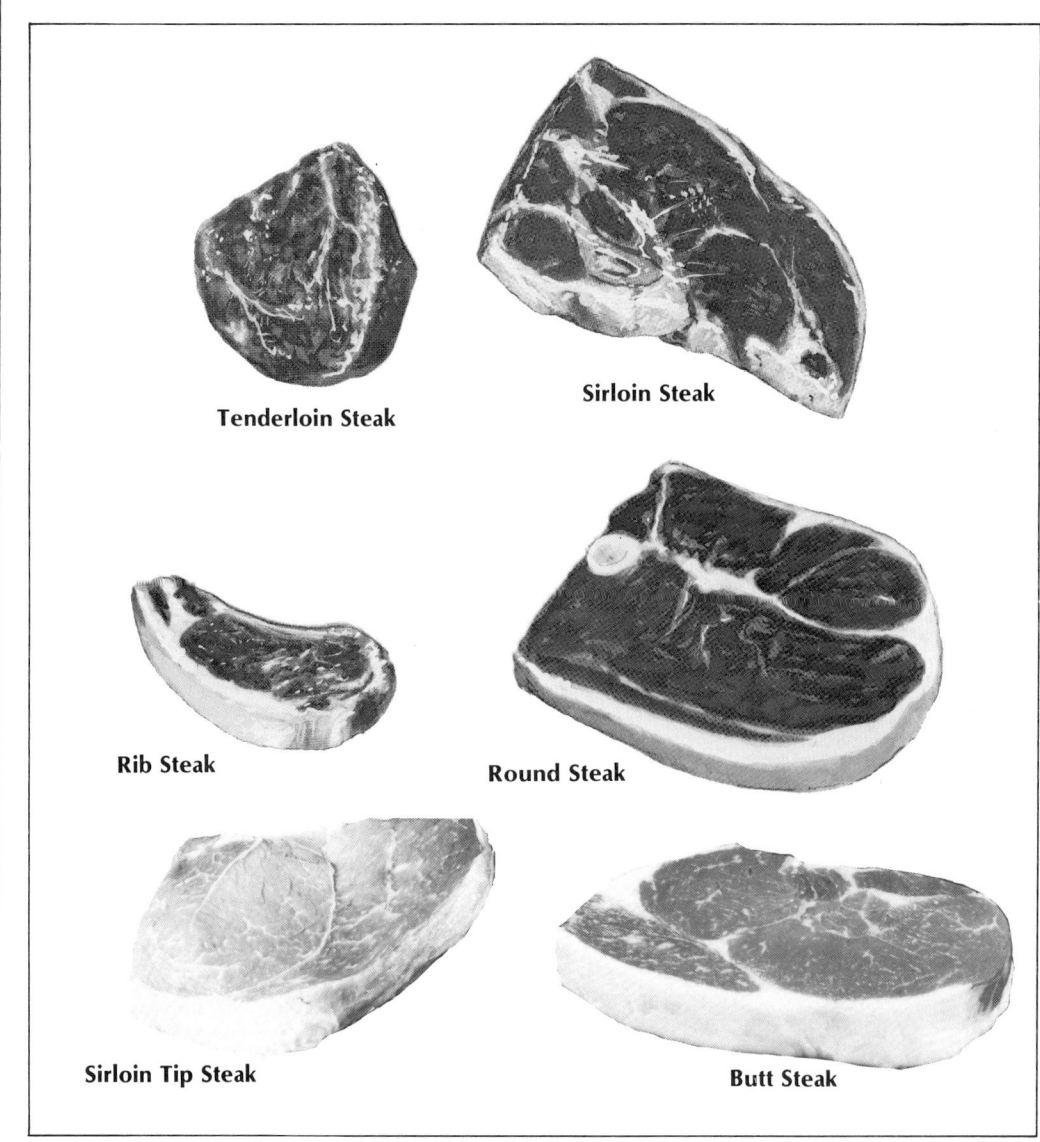

Tenderloin Steak Sirloin Steak

Rib Steak Round Steak

Sirloin Tip Steak Butt Steak

BEEF ROASTS FOR SPIT AND GRILL

Most beef roasts are suitable for barbecuing. The larger roasts are best for spit cooking, while flat roasts such as chuck and brisket may be cooked right on the grill.

Standing Rib Roast: A great favorite for cooking on the spit. Be sure to tie and fasten firmly. Allow about 1 pound per person.

Rib Eye Roast: The choice, tender eye muscle of the rib. No bone. Allow ½ pound per person.

Bone Chuck Roast: Marinate and use a meat tenderizer if not a prime grade of meat. Cook right on the grill, turning and basting from time to time. Allow one pound per person.

Sirloin Tip Roast: An economical and tasty roast for spit cooking. There is no bone. Allow ½ pound per person.

Beef Brisket: Cook long and slow in a double sheet of foil on the grill. Allow ¾ pound per person.

Top Round Sirloin Roast: A very tender cut of lean meat. Allow ⅓–½ pound per person.

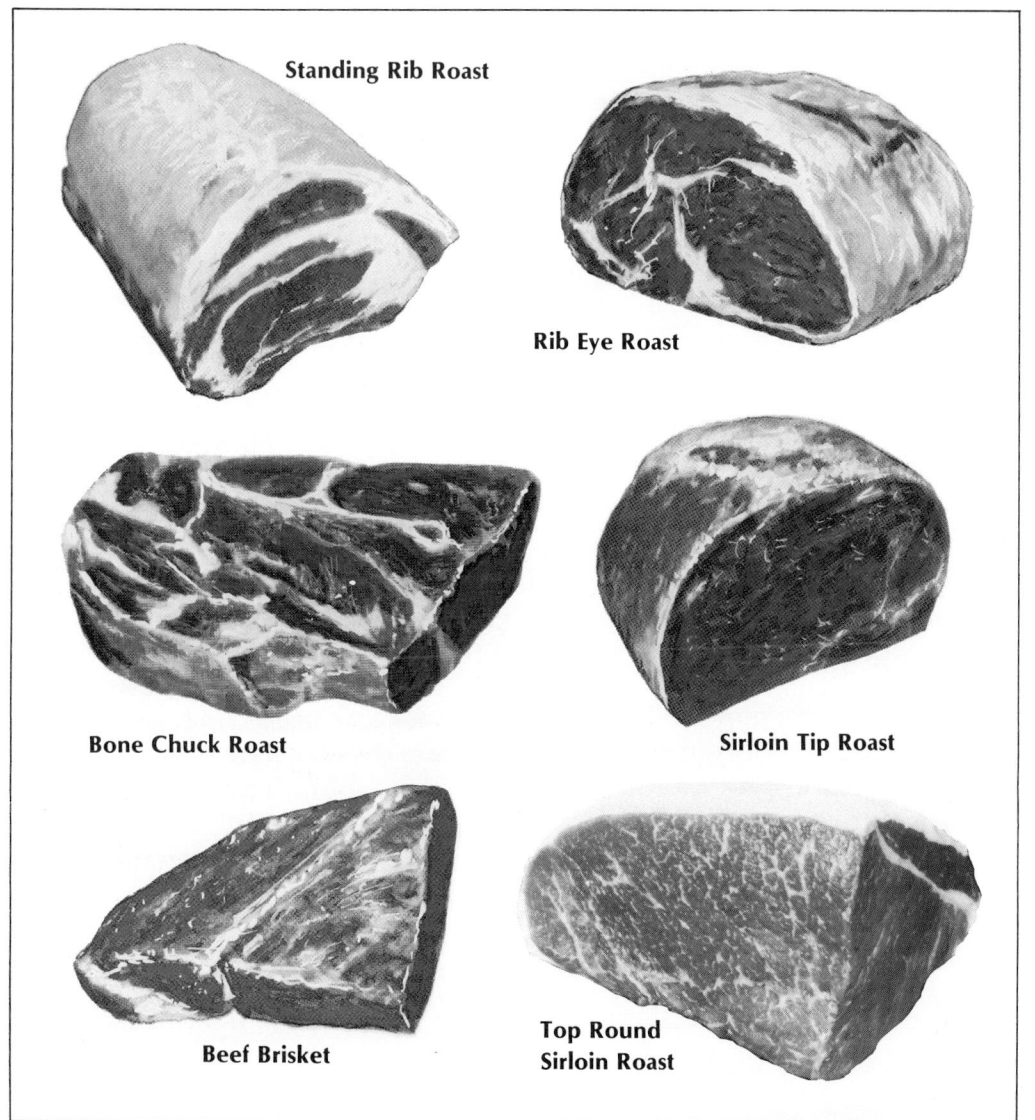

Standing Rib Roast

Rib Eye Roast

Bone Chuck Roast

Sirloin Tip Roast

Beef Brisket

Top Round Sirloin Roast

BEEF

BUTT STEAK WITH VINAIGRETTE LETTUCE

Yield: 2 servings

Heat Control: high, lid closed, direct heat

This recipe can easily be increased for larger servings. A very attractive dish that provides a relief from the traditional steak, baked potato, and salad meal.

Marinade
- 2 tablespoons olive oil
- 2 tablespoons peanut oil
- 2–3 cloves garlic, minced
- 6–7 black peppercorns, crushed
- 1 butt steak, trimmed (about 10 ounces)
- About 2 cups romaine, bibb, or Boston lettuce, or a combination

Lemon Vinaigrette
- 3 tablespoons fresh lemon juice
- 2 tablespoons white or red wine vinegar
- Salt to taste
- ½ teaspoon freshly ground pepper
- ½ teaspoon dry mustard
- ¼ cup olive oil
- ¼ cup peanut oil
- 1 teaspoon Worcestershire sauce
- ⅛ teaspoon garlic powder

For the marinade, put oils, garlic, and peppercorns into a glass baking dish. Place steak on top of marinade; turn to coat. With the back of a spoon, press garlic and peppercorns into steak. Cover with plastic wrap. Let stand at room temperature 4 hours or refrigerate overnight.

Remove steak from marinade. Place steak on grill. Cook on high for 4 minutes, 2 minutes on each side, for rare. (The meat should feel springy to the touch.)

Coarsely shred the lettuce. Put into a large bowl.

For the lemon vinaigrette, whisk lemon juice, wine vinegar, salt, pepper, and mustard until smooth. Gradually whisk in oils until smooth. Just before the steak is finished cooking, stir and pour the vinaigrette over the lettuce; toss to coat. Arrange the greens on a serving platter.

Slice the meat diagonally against the grain, ⅛–¼ inch thick. Arrange the slices over the lettuce in a spoke pattern. Serve immediately.

RANCHO GRANDE STEAK

Yield: 8–10 servings

Heat Control: sear on high, lid open; finish on low, lid closed; direct heat

Even though this is an inexpensive cut of meat, it can be grilled rare, if that's what you prefer. This recipe is an economical as well as a delicious way of serving steak to a large number of people. Leftover meat makes marvelous sandwiches.

- 4 pounds boned top round steak, cut 2 inches thick
- 1 1⅛-ounce package seasoned beef marinade (such as Lawry's)
- ¾ cup dry red wine
- 3 tablespoons lemon juice
- 2 tablespoons salad oil
- ½ teaspoon freshly ground pepper
- ½ teaspoon dried rosemary

Wipe the meat with a damp cloth. Combine all the remaining ingredients in a flat container that is large enough to hold the meat, or

---

To determine if thick steak is done, use a sharp knife and cut a small slit next to the bone or into the thickest part of the steak.

Always have meats, poultry, and seafood at room temperature before cooking. Foods taken directly from the refrigerator to the grill will require longer cooking. Most frozen foods require thawing. Very thin steaks and hamburger patties may be placed on the grill frozen.

put the marinade into a plastic bag. Pierce all surfaces of the meat thoroughly with a sharp pick or a meat fork. Pour the marinade over the meat or put the meat into the plastic bag, seal it securely, and put it into a flat dish. Let stand for 15 minutes, turning the meat once. Drain the meat.

Sear the meat on the grid on high, turning it every 3 minutes, for a total of 12 minutes. Then lower the heat to low and continue cooking for 10 minutes on each side with the lid closed. Use a meat thermometer during the last 10 minutes of cooking so that you can get the exact degree of tenderness you like.

CHOPPED SIRLOIN WITH GREEN ONION

Yield: 6 servings

Heat Control: medium, lid closed, direct heat

These marinated patties can be served plain as well as on a bun.

- 2 pounds chopped or ground sirloin
- ½ cup soy sauce
- 1 cup Burgundy or other dry red wine
- 1 teaspoon celery seed
- 1 teaspoon garlic powder
- 1 teaspoon coarsely ground pepper
- 1 tablespoon finely chopped parsley
- 1 tablespoon finely chopped green onion

Form the meat into 6 patties of equal size and place them in a deep dish. Combine the remaining ingredients and pour over the patties. Marinate 2–3 hours in the refrigerator, turning occasionally. Cook on the grid over medium heat, with the lid closed, 4 minutes per side for medium rare. Because these meat patties have been marinated and contain extra moisture, they will take a bit longer to cook.

CHUCK WAGON STEAK

Yield: 5–7 servings

Heat Control: low, lid closed, direct heat

This is a very tasty way of preparing an economical cut of meat.

**2½ pounds chuck steak, approximately 1 inch thick
Charmglow Bar-B-Q Sauce (see recipe) or commercial barbecue sauce**

Sear the meat on the grid on high, with the lid closed, 2 minutes on each side. Lower the heat on the grill to low. Brush the meat with barbecue sauce on both sides and grill for 20 minutes, turning the meat several times.

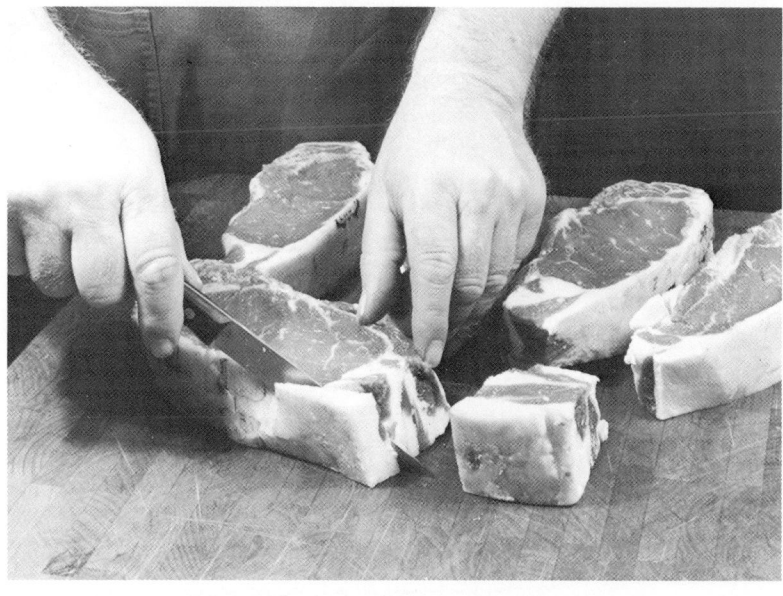

(Below) Be sure to trim thick fat from steaks and chops before grilling. A little fat dripping onto the hot briquets is necessary to obtain the "Barbecue Flavor" but excess drippings may cause flareups.

(Above) Wine marinades tenderize less-tender cuts of meat. Beef, such as blade-cut chuck, picks up flavor after a minimum of 1 hour in the marinade. These cuts may be grill-cooked or pot-roasted wrapped in foil.

ROUND STEAK IN FOIL

Yield: 4–6 servings

Heat Control: low, lid closed, indirect heat

This has a flavor quite similar to that of Swiss steak.

- 2 pounds round steak, 1 inch thick
- 1 cup chili sauce
- ¼ cup water
- ½ teaspoon salt or to taste
- ¼ teaspoon pepper
- 1 teaspoon paprika
- 1 medium onion, sliced
- ½ teaspoon garlic salt
- ½ cup chopped green pepper

Tenderize the steak on both sides with a meat mallet. Mix the chili sauce and water. Combine the remaining ingredients and spoon half of this mixture into the center of a double thickness of aluminum foil that has been sprayed with nonstick vegetable spray. Place steak on top. Cover with the remaining seasoning mixture. Fold the foil over the meat and seal the edges tightly, butcher wrap style. Place on the grill. Cook over low heat for 1 hour and 10 minutes, turning several times with tongs. Twenty minutes before the steak is done, open the package and add water, if needed. Reseal the package and continue cooking. Serve the steak in its own juice, with vegetables as a garnish.

STEAK AU POIVRE (PEPPER STEAK FLAMBÉ)

Yield: Serves 4–6

Heat Control: low, lid closed, direct heat

Often served in very elegant restaurants, this steak with cracked peppercorns has a most unusual flavor.

- 1 tablespoon cracked peppercorns
- 3 pounds boneless sirloin tip steak, ¾–1 inch thick
- Salt to taste
- ¼ cup brandy (optional)
- ¼ cup melted butter

Press cracked peppercorns into both sides of steak and let stand 20–30 minutes. Place steak on a preheated grill. Cook on low, with the lid closed, for 3 minutes per side for medium-rare. Cook for 3½ minutes per side for medium, and 4 minutes per side for well done. Season steak with salt and transfer to a heated platter. Pour warmed brandy over and ignite. When the flame dies, pour melted butter over the steak and serve at once.

Variation: Slice and sauté ½ pound mushrooms in the butter and pour over the meat.

SWISS STEAK PACKET DINNER

Yield: 1 serving

The secret to "Classic Barbecuing" is in the selection of marinades and sauces. Meats may be tenderized as well as flavored with exotic mixtures of wines, oils, herbs, and spices.

Cook rare steaks at the front of the grill and cook medium or well-done steaks at the rear of the grill where heat is more intense.

Heat Control: low, lid closed, direct heat and then warming shelf

These are fun to make and serve to a group. Your guests can cook their own when they like. You can also make a lot of them at one time and freeze some for later use.

- 1 tablespoon flour
- 6 ounces round steak (see note below)
- 1 carrot, cut into strips
- 1 small onion, quartered
- 1 small potato, pared and cut into strips
- 2 green pepper rings
- ¼ cup chopped celery
- 1 tablespoon plus 1 teaspoon ketchup
- ¼ teaspoon salt
- ⅛ teaspoon pepper
- 1 tablespoon dry red wine or water

Pound the flour into the steak with a meat mallet to tenderize and place on a square of double-thick heavy-duty aluminum foil. Arrange the vegetables on and around the steak. Top with the remaining ingredients, sprinkling with wine or water. Wrap securely and place on the grill. Cook on low, with the lid closed, for 20–25 minutes, then on the warming shelf for another 20–25 minutes, with the lid closed.

Note: In order to save time, if you do not wish to tenderize the meat with a meat mallet, have your butcher tenderize it with a cuber machine.

GAUCHO THICK STEAK

Yield: 8 servings

Heat Control: sear on high and finish on low, lid closed, direct heat

The brandy marinade in this recipe gives the meat a delicate flavor usually found in more complicated dishes.

- **2–3 pounds top sirloin steak, 2 inches thick**
- ¼ **cup brandy**
- **Pepper to taste**
- ½ **pound fresh mushrooms, sliced**
- ½ **cup vinegar-oil dressing**

Pierce the entire surface of the meat with a two-pronged meat fork on both sides. Marinate the steak in brandy about 30 minutes to 1 hour, turning several times.

Place the mushrooms in a shallow bowl and marinate in vinegar-oil dressing. Sear the steaks on the grid on high, with the lid closed, for 2 minutes on each side. Decrease the heat to low and continue grilling on both sides. Remove the steak when done to your taste. Use tongs to place on a heated serving platter or a carving board. Slice into ½-inch diagonal pieces. Drain the mushrooms and serve over the meat. Serve immediately.

(Below) Arrange steaks or chops so that the thickest portion is towards the center. Always turn steaks with tongs to avoid loss of natural juices. Season steaks after cooking as salt tends to draw moisture from meats.

RUM STEAK

Yield: 6 servings (½ pound per person)
Heat Control: low, lid closed, direct heat

Overnight marinating gives this meat a strong, distinctive flavor.

3	pounds steak, 1½ inches thick (T-bone, porterhouse, sirloin, or other tender cut)
½	cup rum
2	cloves garlic, crushed
1	teaspoon grated ginger or ½ teaspoon powdered ginger
1	cup soy sauce

Place the meat in a shallow dish. Combine the remaining ingredients and pour over the steak. Marinate overnight, in refrigerator. Remove meat from marinade and reserve liquid. Marinade is sufficient to marinate 3 pounds of steak. Cook on the grid with the lid closed, 2½ minutes per side for rare, 3 minutes per side for medium rare, 3½ minutes per side for medium, or to your taste, basting with the marinade during cooking.

SALISBURY STEAKS WITH ROQUEFORT

Yield: 4 servings
Heat Control: low, lid closed, direct heat

Give a French flavor to your hamburgers.

2	pounds ground round or chuck
¼	teaspoon pepper
¼	cup dry red wine
1	tablespoon finely chopped onion
	Salt to taste
4	ounces Roquefort cheese

Combine all the ingredients except cheese. Shape the meat into 8 patties, each about ¼ inch thick. Divide the cheese into 4 equal portions and place on top of 4 of the patties. Place the remaining patties on top of the cheese patties. Press the meat together, sealing the edges. Cook on the grid on low, with the lid closed, for 4 minutes on each side. Patties are about 1 inch thick after being put together.

GRILLED MINUTE STEAK

Yield: 4 servings
Heat Control: high, lid closed, direct heat

A real quickie! Searing these steaks on high seals in juices. They also seem more tender than when cooked at a lower temperature.

½	cup melted butter or margarine
1	tablespoon lemon juice
2	tablespoons minced parsley
1	tablespoon minced chives
4	minute steaks or cubed steaks, ¼–½ inch thick

Salt and pepper to taste
Toasted onion or sesame rolls

Mix the butter, lemon juice, parsley, and chives together and coat steaks. Place on the grill. Cook for 2 minutes on high, with the lid closed, brushing frequently with the butter mixture. Season with salt and pepper. Serve on toasted onion or sesame rolls.

SIRLOIN STEAK WITH CHARMGLOW MARINADE

Yield: ⅓–½ pound per person
Heat Control: sear on high and finish on medium, lid closed, direct heat

This marinade tenderizes as well as flavors steak.

A chef determines the doneness of grilled steaks with a finger. A rare steak will feel soft. Medium will be partly firm. Well done will feel firm. Also, natural juices will appear when steaks are pressed. Red juice indicates rare, pink means medium, and broth color signals well done.

Always have the lid open when lighting a gas barbecue.

1–2 pounds thick sirloin tip steak
Charmglow Marinade for Steak (see recipe)

Pierce the entire steak with a meat fork. Marinate the steak for 30 minutes, 15 minutes per side. Sear on the grid on high for 2 minutes on each side, with the lid closed. Reduce the heat to medium and continue cooking for additional 13 minutes for rare (6½ minutes per side), with lid closed. Baste several times during cooking, after searing.

MEAL-IN-ONE CHUCK ROAST

Yield: 6 servings

Heat Control: sear on high, lid closed, and finish on low, lid open 1 inch, indirect heat

An economical and quick way to cook vegetables and meat in one dish!

3–5 pounds beef chuck roast
1 teaspoon seasoned salt
1 large onion, sliced
6 medium potatoes, quartered lengthwise
6 large carrots, peeled or scraped
¼ cup cooking oil
1 cup ketchup
¼ cup water
½ teaspoon pepper
1 teaspoon dry mustard
¼ cup soy sauce
2 tablespoons wine vinegar

Brown the roast on a hot grill (high) about 15 minutes on each side. Remove the roast and place it on a large sheet of double-thick aluminum foil. Place the sliced onion on top, and the potatoes and carrots around the roast. Combine the remaining ingredients in a saucepan. Cook slowly over the grill, stirring constantly until the mixture comes to a boil. Do not boil. Pour over the roast and vegetables. Wrap the foil securely around the roast, sealing the edges well. Place on the grill. Cook at low for 1¼ hours with lid in the 1-inch position, or until done. Turn with tongs several times.

ROLLED BONELESS BEEF ROAST

Yield: 6–8 servings

Heat Control: low, lid closed, rotisserie

This roast is delicious, with just a hint of garlic and herbs.

5–6 pounds rolled beef roast
1 small onion, slivered
2 garlic cloves, slivered
1 teaspoon thyme
Pepper to taste
2 tablespoons olive oil
2 tablespoons dry vermouth

Make several incisions in the surface of the meat and insert slivers of onion and garlic. Rub the roast with thyme and pepper. Brush the surface of the roast with a little of the olive oil. Combine the remaining oil and vermouth and set aside. Secure the roast on a spit. Cook on low, approximately 23 minutes per pound for rare, with the lid closed. You may wish to raise the cover to the 2-inch position during the last 30–45 minutes if the meat is getting too dark on the outside and the proper internal temperature has not yet been reached on the meat thermometer. Baste the meat frequently with the vermouth marinade during the final 30 minutes of cooking. Let the roast sit for 10–15 minutes before carving. Slice thin.

A barbecue flavor is obtained with a gas-fired grill when fats and cooking juices hit the hot briquets and create aromatic smoke that envelops foods being cooked.

MEAT LOAF IN FOIL

Yield: 4 servings

Heat Control: low, lid closed, warming shelf

Grilled baked potatoes are a nice accompaniment to this economical entrée.

- 2 pounds ground beef
- ¼ pound ground pork
- 1 cup breadcrumbs
- ¾ cup vegetable juice or tomato juice
- 1 egg, lightly beaten
- ¼ cup minced onion
- 2 tablespoons minced parsley
- ¼ teaspoon thyme
- 1 teaspoon salt or to taste
- ½ teaspoon pepper or to taste
- 6 drops Tabasco sauce

Mix the meats with the remaining ingredients and shape into a loaf. Place on a double thickness of heavy-duty aluminum foil that has been coated inside with cooking oil or sprayed with a nonstick vegetable spray. Wrap edges securely and place on the warming shelf. Cook on low, with the lid closed, for approximately 1 hour. Using tongs, gently turn the meat loaf several times. Slice and serve with your favorite barbecue sauce or chili sauce. For a stronger barbecue flavor, open the foil during the last 20 minutes of cooking.

ROAST BRISKET OF CORNED BEEF

Yield: about 6 servings

Heat Control: low (1 burner), lid closed, indirect heat

Corned beef lovers will be delighted with this variation, as it has a very nice crusty layer on the outside, yet is moist and tender on the inside.

- 1 piece of corned beef brisket, approximately 3–4 lbs.

Brisket is best cooked slowly over low heat. Use only 1 burner, with the lid closed. Place the brisket on a roasting rack or in an aluminum foil pan and cook on low for about 15 minutes per pound. When the meat seems tender, remove it from the grill and let it stand for 10 minutes for easier carving.

GRILLED VEAL CUTLETS

Yield: 4–6 servings

Heat Control: low, lid closed, direct heat

You'll be amazed at how delicious and tender these cutlets are.

- 2 pounds veal cutlets, sliced ⅛- to ¼-inch thick
- Juice of 2 lemons
- 1 tablespoon minced chives or shallots
- 2 tablespoons minced parsley
- ½ clove garlic, crushed
- ⅓ cup melted butter or cooking oil
- Salt and pepper to taste

With a meat hammer, wooden mallet, or edge of a plate, pound cutlets to tenderize them. Place veal in a shallow pan. Mix the remaining ingredients and pour over the meat. Marinate at least 2 hours, turning frequently. Place the cutlets on the grill. Cook at low, with the lid closed, 4–5 minutes per side, basting with the remaining marinade.

ROMANO VEAL PATTIES

Yield: 6 servings
Heat Control: medium, lid closed, direct heat

Because veal is very lean, there are no fat drippings to fuel the fire. As a consequence, these patties take longer to cook than other meats of the same thickness.

- 2 pounds chopped or ground veal
- ½ teaspoon anchovy paste
- 1 clove garlic, minced or pressed
- 1 teaspoon olive oil
- ¼ teaspoon salt
- ¼ teaspoon pepper
- ¼ teaspoon oregano or Italian seasoning
- Mozzarella cheese (optional)

Combine meat with seasonings. Shape into 6 equal-sized patties, about ¾ inch thick. Place on the grill. Cook on medium, with lid closed, for 7 minutes on each side.

Variation: During the last minute of cooking, place a slice of mozzarella cheese on top of each patty.

LAMB

Most people tend to overcook lamb, which ruins the texture as well as the flavor. Place a meat thermometer in the largest muscle of the roast, not touching a bone. Consult the following chart for proper cooking temperatures:

Cooking Time for Lamb
Rare—140°F.
Medium-rare—160°F.
Well done—170-180°F.

LAMB CHOPS

Yield: 4 servings
Heat Control: low, lid closed, direct heat

Lamb at its best.

- 8 lean loin lamb chops, about ½ inch thick
- Lemon juice
- Herbs (optional)
- Salt and pepper

Slit the fat at the edge of the chops to prevent curling. Sprinkle with lemon juice and sprinkle with herbs of your choice, if desired. Oregano, basil, and garlic powder, are good choices. Cook on the grid on low, 5 minutes on each side, with the lid closed, or until it is done to your taste. Salt and pepper as desired. Serve immediately.

WILD RICE DRESSING

This is a delicious and easy-to-make dressing, good with pork and poultry dishes, too.

- 1 6¾-ounce package Uncle Ben's Wild Rice mixture
- ¼ pound pork sausage
- ½ cup chopped celery
- ½ cup chopped onion
- ¼ cup chopped parsley
- 1 8-ounce can water chestnuts
- ¼ cup coarsely chopped pecans (optional)

Cook rice according to package directions. Cook pork sausage in a small skillet and drain. Then combine the sausage with the rice and remaining ingredients. Heat through before serving.

CROWN ROAST OF LAMB

Yield: 4–6 servings

Heat Control: low, lid closed, indirect heat

For a spectacular and truly elegant meal, try this lamb roast. Heat the stuffing separately in a heavy crock or casserole dish on the grill or in your oven. Fill the center after it has been placed on the serving platter or carving board.

- 1 4½- to 5-pound crown lamb roast
- ⅓ cup lemon juice
- 2 teaspoons oregano
- ¼ teaspoon garlic powder
- Salt and pepper to taste

Be sure the butcher has tied the roast securely. Bone ends may be frenched (meat cut back away from bone about 1 inch), if colored paper "panties" for serving decoration are desired. Combine lemon juice, oregano, garlic powder, and pepper. Brush the roast with the lemon juice mixture. Place the roast in an aluminum foil pan, heavy or meaty side down, or prepare a double-thick foil drip pan a little larger than the roast bottom. Cook at low for 45 minutes, with the lid closed. Insert a meat thermometer during the last 15 minutes of cooking. Lamb is done when it reaches 140–145° F. Salt as desired.

ROAST LEG OF LAMB WITH HERB STUFFING

Yield: 8–10 servings

Heat Control: low, lid closed, rotisserie

Garlic and oregano in this recipe permeate the entire roast, giving it a marvelous flavor.

- 1 leg of lamb, 7–9 pounds
- ¾ cup chopped fresh parsley
- 6–8 small cloves garlic, minced, or 1 teaspoon garlic powder
- 1 tablespoon oregano
- Grated rind of 1 lemon
- ½ teaspoon salt
- Dash crushed red pepper
- Juice of 1 lemon

Have the butcher bone the leg of lamb for stuffing. Have him tell you the boned weight so you can calculate the cooking time. Mix parsley, garlic, oregano, grated lemon rind, salt, and red pepper. Open up the leg of lamb; spread with parsley mixture. Roll up; tie securely in several places with kitchen string. Secure on the spit with holding forks. Place the rotisserie on the grill with heat set at low, lid closed, and cook for approximately 15 minutes per pound. Baste with lemon juice. Use a meat thermometer. Lamb is best when served medium-rare

(Below) Thread meat loosely on skewers to insure even browning. Kebabs may be marinated in a variety of sauces to tenderize and flavor.

(140–145° F.) For easier carving, let the roast sit for 10 minutes before serving.

MUSHROOM-STUFFED LAMB CHOPS

Yield: 6 servings

Heat Control: medium, lid closed or open, direct heat or rotisserie basket

Even those who do not love lamb will appreciate the taste and appearance of these chops.

- 2 tablespoons finely chopped shallots
- 2 tablespoons snipped parsley
- 1 tablespoon chopped green pepper
- 1 tablespoon chopped fresh basil or ½ teaspoon dried basil
- ½ pound mushrooms, chopped
- 3 tablespoons butter, preferably clarified
- ⅔ cup soft breadcrumbs
- ¼ teaspoon salt
- Dash freshly ground pepper
- 6 large loin lamb chops, 1½ inches thick, with pocket

Sauté shallots, parsley, green pepper, basil, and mushrooms in butter for 5 minutes. Remove from heat; stir in breadcrumbs, salt, and pepper. Wipe chops and trim of any excess fat. Stuff each pocket with as much mushroom mixture as possible. Fasten with wooden picks. If pockets aren't extended all the way to the bone, take a sharp boning knife and extend them to the bone. You can stuff these ahead and refrigerate to this point. Place in a rotisserie basket, grill on medium heat with the lid closed for 12 minutes, or on direct heat for 10 minutes, turning a couple of times during the cooking.

LAMB SHISH KEBAB

Yield: 4–6 servings

Heat Control: low, lid closed, direct heat

Serve this over rice. Vegetables on a skewer (see recipe for Basted Garden Vegetables) make a nice accompaniment.

- 3 pounds lean lamb, cut into 1¼-inch cubes
- ½ cup olive oil
- ¼ cup lemon juice
- 1 teaspoon dried mint
- ½ teaspoon oregano
- 1 teaspoon salt
- ¼ teaspoon pepper
- 2 tablespoons finely chopped onion

Place the lamb in a shallow dish. Combine the remaining ingredients and pour over the meat. Marinate at least 8 hours, or overnight, in the refrigerator. Thread meat loosely on skewers. Place on the grill. Cook on low, with the lid closed, for 6 minutes on each side, or until done to your taste. Brush frequently with the remaining marinade. Take care not to overcook. Lamb should be slightly pink on inside.

Variation: You may wish to use the marinade for Armenian Chicken (see recipe) for a different flavor.

PORK

After extensive research, Iowa State University, along with several other universities and in conjunction with the National Livestock and Meat Board, now recommends an internal temperature of 170° F., rather than 185° F., for all fresh pork roasts.

Meat on skewers: Meat should be threaded loosely on skewers so that basting sauce and heat can penetrate meat evenly.

In cold weather, always preheat the gas barbecue at high for five minutes to obtain a satisfactory cooking temperature. Adjust the heat to medium or low after preheating.

Fully thawed meat should be roasted at a low temperature. The results show that pork roast cooked to a final internal temperature of 170° F. is comparable in flavor and tenderness, higher in juiciness, and has a lower moisture loss than pork roasted to an internal temperature of 185° F. Another advantage is the shorter cooking time required. For pork roasts, the roasting time can be shortened as much as 6–8 minutes per pound.

Some meat thermometers are marked with these new temperatures; however, some are not. So make a mental note of these temperature changes the next time you're preparing a pork roast.

ORIENTAL SPARERIBS

Yield: 4–6 servings

Heat Control: low, lid open and then closed to the 2-inch position, direct heat or rotisserie

For those who like their ribs with a charred flavor, the direct heat method is recommended.

4–6 pounds back ribs, country ribs, or lean spareribs
Barbecue Sauce for Oriental Spareribs (see recipe)

Place the ribs on the grill, bone side down, or thread on a spit. On the grill, cook on low, with the lid open, for about 45 minutes, turning frequently, until all fat burns off; then close the lid to the 2-inch position. Combine the sauce ingredients and brush over the ribs, cooking for an additional 20 minutes, or until the ribs are done (meat will pull away from end of rib bone). Continue basting and turning for even flavor and to prevent searing. For those that like a less charred taste, use an indirect method like the rotisserie. Serve with additional sauce.

BARBECUED RIBS

Heat Control: low (1 burner), lid closed, indirect heat

The best way to grill all ribs is via indirect heat. All types of ribs—spareribs, back ribs, country ribs, etc.—are best prepared in this

Cooking Time for Ribs

Spareribs	2 hours*	Low	1 burner
Backribs	3 hours	Low	1 burner
Country ribs (3" thick)	3 hours	Low	1 burner

*If you like your meat to fall off the bone, cook for an additional 20 minutes. On smaller grills you may wish to prop the lid open 1 inch.

manner. Generally speaking, a very slow method of cooking helps render all the fat from ribs and at the same time tenderizes the meat. With this method of cooking you can easily give your ribs a wonderful smoke flavor and/or brush with barbecue sauce. You can brush the barbecue sauce on ribs at the start of cooking without worrying that the sauce will burn.

Ignite only 1 burner. Add hickory chips or mesquite, in foil packages, if desired.

Put a shallow foil drip pan under the grids on the unlit side of the grill. Fill the drip pan with water. Trim excess fat from the meat. Place all your meat on this half of the grill. Ribs can overlap if you are preparing a large quantity. Close the lid. Ribs with a nice smoke flavor are often enjoyed without any kind of sauce, or you can serve barbecue sauce on the side. Ribs will be nicely browned and very tender.

If you enjoy sauce on your ribs, brush it on the meat at the beginning. Then baste and turn every 30 minutes. The turning is important, as it allows the rendered fat to drip or run off the meat. Check the drip pan from time to time, making sure that the bottom of the pan is covered with water at all times.

SPARERIBS ON A SPIT

Yield: 3–7 servings (about ¾ pound each for moderate appetites and 1–1¼ pounds for hearty appetites)
Heat Control: low, lid closed, rotisserie

For people who like to cook pork ribs slowly on a spit, we recommend this slow cooking method.

4–5 pounds lean spareribs
Barbecue sauce

Trim any excess fat from the ribs. Thread the spareribs on a spit, making sure that they are secure and properly balanced. Spareribs can be folded back and forth in an accordion pattern with the spit going through the center. A larger piece of meat with a high fat content may change its balance as it cooks. Place a drip pan under the spit and fill with water. Cook on low, with lid closed, for 30–35 minutes. Ribs should be nicely browned and almost done. Continue cooking for an additional 15–20 minutes, basting every 5 minutes with the sauce of your choice. Sweet and Sour Sauce (see recipe) is especially good. You may wish to serve additional sauce at the table for dipping. Simmer on the stove for about 10 minutes so that it becomes more concentrated for dipping. Traditional barbecue sauce can also be used. Either make your own recipe or use a commercial barbecue sauce (such as Open Pit).

(Below) Whole sparerib sections should be trimmed of excess fat and placed on barbecue skewer "accordion style." Use a foil drip pan to catch drippings. Baste during final 15 minutes of cooking.

If meat or poultry is getting too dark on the outside, and proper temperature has not been reached on the thermometer, raise the barbecue cover to the 2-inch position.

Exotic barbecue flavors may be obtained by seasoning the hot briquets with wet wood chips wrapped in heavy-duty foil in a cylinderlike shape, leaving the ends open. Place these foil packets directly on the Charm-Rok toward the front or the coolest part of your grill.

SPIT-ROASTED ROLLED PORK ROAST

Yield: 4–6 servings

Heat Control: low, lid closed, indirect heat (rotisserie optional)

A basting sauce in this recipe imparts a lovely fruity flavor to the herbed pork roast.

1 3- to 4-pound rolled pork roast
Pepper to taste
Garlic powder (optional)
Herbs of your choice (oregano, basil, etc.)
Pork Basting Sauce (see recipe)

Insert a drip pan into your grill. Skewer a rolled pork roast evenly on the spit or set on a roasting rack. Cook at low, with the lid closed, approximately 30 minutes per pound. Baste the meat during the last 20 minutes of cooking. Use a meat thermometer to determine when it is done.

SMOKED PORK CHOPS

Yield: 1 pork chop per person

Heat Control: high, lid closed, direct heat

Smoked pork chops are a favorite in many areas of the country. They can be cooked quickly and succulently on your grill, following this recipe.

¾-inch-thick smoked pork chops

Because smoked pork chops are already cooked, they just need to be heated through. Heat the grill to high. Cook the smoked pork chops for 2 minutes per side on high, with the lid closed.

GRILLED PORK CHOPS

Yield: 1 chop per person

Heat Control: low, lid closed, direct heat

Pork chops that are one-inch thick or thicker are best for grilling. Thinner pork chops tend to dry out.

1-inch-thick center-cut pork chops
Salt or garlic salt to taste
Pepper to taste
Barbecue Sauce (optional)

Score the fat on the pork chops so they don't curl up. Place on the grill and cook on low, with the lid closed, for about 25–30 minutes, or until they are browned on both sides. Turn often to keep juices in and to prevent burning them. Season to taste with salt and pepper. Garlic salt is also good on pork chops.

Variation: You may also brush the chops with your favorite barbecue sauce during the last 5 minutes, turning occasionally.

MANDARIN PORK

Yield: 8–10 servings

Heat Control: low (2 burners), lid closed, indirect heat

This dish from Northern China is easy to make.

4–4½ pounds boneless top loin pork roast
4 scallions
1 long slice fresh ginger root
3 drops red food coloring
1 tablespoon soy sauce
2 tablespoons dry sherry
4 tablespoons sugar
½ teaspoon garlic powder

2 tablespoons ketchup
1 tablespoon Hoisin sauce (see note below)

Basting Sauce
1 tablespoon honey
1 tablespoon orange juice
½ tablespoon lemon juice

Cut meat in half along the grain. Cut scallions into 2-inch pieces and crush. Do the same with the ginger. Combine the remaining ingredients with the ginger and scallions and pour the marinade over the meat. Marinate for 6 hours or overnight. Preheat the grill. Cook via the indirect method, either on a roasting rack or in a foil pan. Brush the sauce on the meat and roast about 30 minutes per pound, or until a meat thermometer registers done.

Note: Hoisin sauce may be purchased in any Oriental store and in many supermarkets in 1-pound jars or cans. It keeps well and adds a unique flavor to many dishes.

PORK SIRLOIN ROAST

Yield: 8–10 servings (½ pound per person because of bone)

Heat Control: Low (1 burner), lid closed, indirect heat

This roast is a bit difficult to carve because of the bone, but it's worth it for the flavor.

1   4- to 5-pound lean pork sirloin roast with bone in
Caraway seed
Dried dill

Sprinkle the pork sirloin roast generously with caraway seed and dried dill. Place a roasting rack in an aluminum foil pan to which water has been added. Place roast on rack. Cook on low, with the lid closed, for 40 minutes per pound. Baste with the pan drippings during the last 45 minutes of cooking.

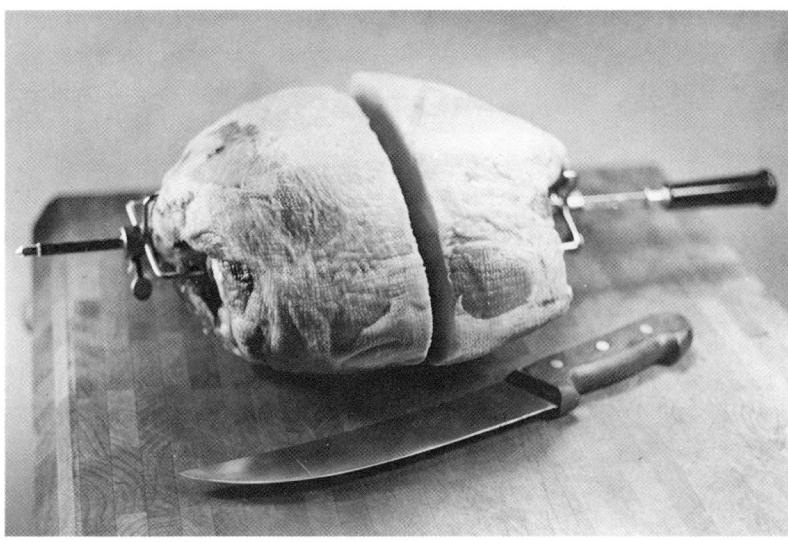

(Above) Whole bone in hams are partially cooked in curing. They require only heating. For best results have butcher cut ham in two and spit cook with space between halves for quick and easy heating.

ROLLED PORK ROAST

Yield: 9–12 servings (⅓ pound per person)

Heat Control: low (1 burner), lid closed, indirect heat

This roast is cooked via indirect heat—a convenient cooking method that leaves you with half a grill on which to cook some additional meats or accompaniments such as vegetables.

1   3- to 4-pound rolled pork roast
1   recipe Sweet and Sour Table Sauce (see recipe)

Cook roast on low, with the lid closed, approximately 29 minutes per pound. Baste with Sweet and Sour Table Sauce.

Ham

BONELESS HAM

Yield: 6–15 servings (⅓–½ pound per serving)

Heat Control: low, lid closed, rotisserie

Hams are partially cooked during curing, so they require only heating. Use a meat thermometer to make sure the ham is heated through; usually 140–150° F. is sufficient.

1   3- to 5-pound boneless ham
Whole cloves
Sweet and Sour Basting Sauce (see recipe)

Score the entire surface of the ham and dot it decoratively with whole cloves. Skewer the ham on a spit; check the balance. Place a shallow drip pan underneath the meat and fill it with water. Cook for 45 minutes to an hour, depending on the size of the ham. Continue cooking an additional 15–20 minutes, basting every 5 minutes. When the ham is at the proper temperature, transfer it to a carving board and serve.

Variation: Ham can also be cooked on a roasting rack with a drip pan underneath.

SPIT GRILLED HAM

Yield: 8–10 servings

Heat Control: low, lid closed

You'll be amazed at the wonderful clove flavor that delicately permeates the ham.

1   6½- to 7-pound whole ham with bone in (at room temperature)
Whole cloves

Score fat on outside of ham, and place whole cloves in scored sections. Skewer ham on spit, making sure it balances properly. Place drip pan underneath meat. Cook on low, lid closed, for approximately 40 minutes (6-6½ minutes per pound), or until meat thermometer reads 140°. Because ham is cured, it need only be reheated before serving.

LUAU CHOPPED STEAK

Yield: 4 servings

Heat Control: low, lid closed, direct heat

This is very pretty to look at and is a fantastic way to use leftover ham.

1   8¼-ounce can pineapple slices
1   pound chopped smoked ham
1   teaspoon soy sauce
⅛   teaspoon pepper
½   cup ketchup
¼   cup brown sugar
2   tablespoons Worcestershire sauce

Drain the pineapple, saving about 2 tablespoons of the juice. Season the meat with soy sauce and pepper and shape it into thick patties. Press a pineapple slice firmly into each patty, sealing around the edges of the slice so it does not fall out during cooking. Make a sauce of the reserved pineapple juice, ketchup, brown sugar, and Worcestershire sauce heated together. Brush on the patties and place them on the grill. Cook on low, with the lid closed, 5 minutes per side, or until done to your taste. Brush often with sauce during cooking.

EAST INDIAN SATÉ

Yield: 6–8 entrée servings; 12 or more appetizer servings

Heat Control: low, lid closed, indirect heat (rotisserie basket optional)

This thick marinade has a mild peanut flavor that is delicious with pork, veal, or chicken. The remaining marinade may be served as a sauce over the cooked meat. Traditionally, saté is cooked and served on thin bamboo skewers (see variation at end of recipe).

1 tablespoon ground coriander
¼ teaspoon salt
½ teaspoon freshly ground pepper
1 cup chopped onion
2 cloves garlic, peeled
½ cup soy sauce
¼ cup lemon or lime juice
½ cup peanut butter
¼ cup brown sugar
½ cup peanut or salad oil
Dash cayenne or Tabasco sauce
2 pounds meat (lean boned pork, boned veal leg or shoulder, or boned chicken), cut into 1-inch cubes

Combine all ingredients except meat and whirl until smooth in a blender or food processor. Marinate the meat in this mixture for 1–2 hours. Thread on bamboo skewers. Place in a rotisserie basket over low heat with the lid closed, for 12 minutes, until brown but not dry. Serve with the remaining marinade. If you do not have a grill basket, cook over indirect heat or on a warming shelf, as this marinade tends to burn before the meat is cooked.

Variation: Alternate the meat with chunks of pineapple that have been dipped in melted butter.

Soak wooden skewers in water for an hour or more before threading meat on them and grilling.

Poultry

5

56 The Complete Barbecue Cookbook

Poultry and barbecue cooking were made for each other. Virtually all poultry is tender and requires a minimum of cooking. Quick cooking, coupled with an endless variety of marinades, sauces, and seasonings, offers the barbecue chef a chance to develop really personal specialties.

Yesterday's outdoor cooks generally overpowered the delicate flavor of poultry with traditional spicy tomato sauce. Today's barbecue specialist has discovered the subtle rewards of combining poultry with wines, herbs, and covered slow cooking.

Chicken, either whole or cut into parts, is the most versatile type of poultry. It's also inexpensive and allows the barbecue cook to feed a gang easily and on a budget. Usually chickens are well dressed by the butcher, but care should be taken to trim away excess fat. Select chickens for plumpness and freshness. Allow about ½ chicken per average serving.

Chicken may be seasoned just before cooking. If marinades are used, an hour is adequate since no tenderizing is required.

Spit-cooked poultry should be trussed with twine. Then securely attach the poultry to the spit rod with tines, making sure they are properly balanced. If not properly secured, flopping parts or a loose bird may end up in the briquets, as chicken becomes soft and tender during cooking.

Parts of chicken, Cornish hens, game birds, and turkey may be cooked directly on the grill or in a

(Right) Game hens should be trussed securely. Arrange birds at right angles on the spit to ensure even balance. Extra spit tines are handy when cooking more than one bird.

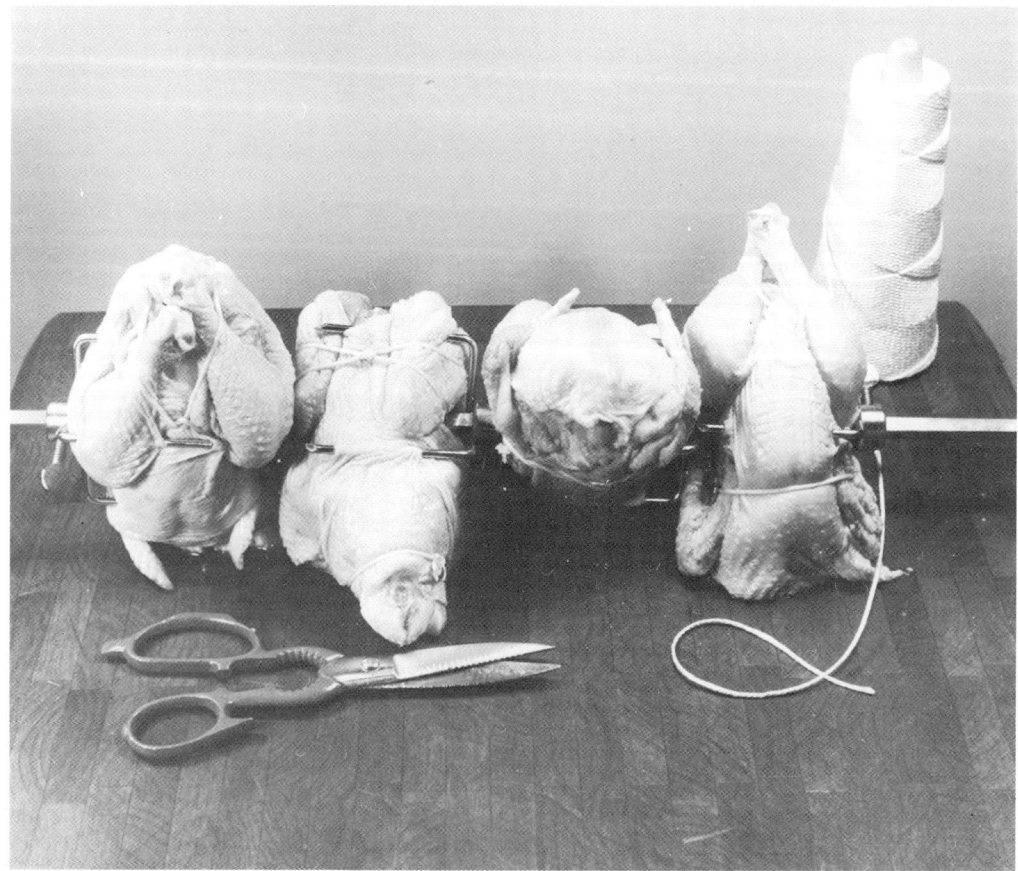

Spit-roasted game hens become a family favorite and may be barbecued at the same time with the rest of your menu. An orange-ginger glaze seals the birds and imparts a delicate flavor.

Take care not to overcook shrimp, as they will become tough. Firm vegetables such as red and green peppers are best precooked or blanched before threading on skewers with the shrimp.

rotisserie basket. Whole poultry is best roasted on a spit or roasting rack. Several chickens or Cornish hens may be spit-cooked at once. Whole turkeys should be limited to eight to 10 pounds for best results on your rotisserie. Larger turkeys can be split and cooked in halves or roasted on a rack with a drip pan underneath.

All poultry is best cooked on low. A meat thermometer should be used to determine doneness in larger birds. Insert the thermometer into the thickest part of breast. Smaller pieces are done when no pink juices appear when the flesh is pricked, and in whole birds when the leg joints turn loosely in their sockets.

Unlike steaks, poultry may be barbecued ahead and warmed on the grill or in a microwave oven prior to serving. This makes it a good selection for large gatherings.

Indirect cooking can be done with one or two burners. When grilling a large turkey, several chickens or a large amount of meat, it's best using two burners so that heat distribution is even. Meat tends to cook more rapidly on one side of the grill, when just one burner is used, causing half the meat to cook quicker and/or burn before remaining meat is done.

(Below) Arrange chicken parts loosely in a spit basket, with the heaviest pieces at the outside edges. Baste chicken frequently during cooking to retain moisture and improve flavor.

CHARMGLOW BASKET CHICKEN

Yield: 4 servings

Heat Control: low, lid closed, rotisserie basket (rotisserie spit for variation)

Quick, moist, and delicious! By using a rotisserie spit or basket, you eliminate constant watching. Also, constantly turning the meat helps flavors penetrate the chicken.

½ cup olive oil
½ cup vinegar
¼ cup dry white wine
½ teaspoon thyme
1 teaspoon oregano
¼ teaspoon hot sauce
1 tablespoon chopped parsley
1 clove garlic, minced
2 2- to 2½-pound chickens, halved

Combine all seasoning ingredients in a saucepan and heat to a boil. Brush the chicken halves with the sauce. Place the halves in an oiled rotisserie basket. Rotisserie-cook at low, with the lid closed, 30–35 minutes, basting frequently.

Variation: Leave the chicken whole and use the spit. Increase the cooking time 10–15 minutes.

BARBECUE ROASTED CHICKEN OR CAPON

Yield: about 3–4 servings

Heat Control: low (2 burners), lid closed, indirect heat

This is a terrific way to serve chicken quickly and economically.

1 3¼-pound chicken or capon
Barbecue sauce

Set the capon on a roasting rack. Set the rack in a foil pan with water. Roast on indirect heat, with lid closed, using both burners (on two burner grill), for approximately 1¼ hours. Brush the capon generously with barbecue sauce during the last 20 minutes of cooking, close the lid, and continue cooking for an additional 10 minutes. Check occasionally to make sure there is still water in the pan.

CHICKEN SHASHLIK

Yield: 4 servings

Heat Control: low, lid closed, direct heat

This marinade really penetrates the chicken, giving it a delightful flavor. Grill vegetables and meat at the same time.

2 whole chicken breasts, skinned and boned
Juice of 2 lemons
1 medium onion, sliced
1 bay leaf
½ cup white wine

- ½ cup olive oil
- 6 peppercorns
- 2 green peppers, cut into 1-inch pieces
- ½ pound mushrooms, stemmed
- ½ pound small onions, peeled

Cut chicken into 1-inch squares. Combine lemon juice, onion, bay leaf, wine, oil, and peppercorns and pour over the chicken. Marinate at least 4 hours or overnight, stirring occasionally. On skewers, thread pieces of chicken, green pepper, mushrooms, and onions. Place on grill and cook at low, with the lid closed, for 12–15 minutes, basting with marinade and turning frequently. This is delicious served over rice.

DELECTABLE CHICKEN IN FOIL

Yield: 4 servings

Heat Control: low, lid closed, warming shelf

Because these delicious chicken packets are cooked on the warming shelf, very little watching is involved.

- 1 3-pound chicken, cut into serving pieces
- 1 envelope onion soup mix
- 1 teaspoon paprika
- 1 4-ounce can mushrooms, drained, or 4 fresh mushrooms
- ¼ cup dry sherry or water
- 4 tablespoons butter

Rinse chicken. Tear off 4 squares of heavy-duty aluminum foil. Blend onion soup mix and paprika in a bowl. Place 1 rounded tablespoon of soup mix in the center of each foil square. Place chicken pieces on top and turn to coat both sides. Add mushrooms and sherry, dividing ingredients evenly among the 4 packages. Dot with butter. Bring foil up over food, sealing the edges with a tight double fold. Place on the warming shelf and cook on low, with the lid closed, for 30 minutes or until done.

CHICKEN EPICUREAN (STUFFED CHICKEN)

Yield: 4–6 servings

Heat Control: low, lid closed, rotisserie

With meat, rice, and vegetables, this is a complete meal in itself!

- ½ cup long-grain rice (not quick-cooking rice)
- ½ cup olive oil
- 1 pound ground lamb, beef, or pork
- ¼ cup slivered almonds
- ¼ teaspoon ground nutmeg
- 1 egg, beaten
- ¼ teaspoon thyme
- ½ teaspoon salt
- ¼ teaspoon pepper
- 1 onion, finely chopped
- ½ cup finely chopped celery
- 1 tablespoon finely chopped pimiento
- ¼ cup dry vermouth
- ½ cup chicken stock
- 1 5-pound roasting chicken or capon

Parboil rice for 7 minutes and drain. Combine with the remaining ingredients. Stuff into the chicken and truss. Secure the chicken on a spit and check the balance. Tighten the skewers with pliers, if necessary. Cook the chicken on low, with the lid closed, for 1¼ hours, or until done. Chicken with dressing takes 20 minutes per pound on a spit.

If too much liquid is added to chicken in foil packets, chicken will not brown properly.

Because of the many variables such as wind, outdoor temperature, and grill models, always check foil packets every 5 minutes during the last 10–15 minutes of cooking.

Cooking time and temperatures will vary with wind, weather, and lid position. Always use a meat thermometer when cooking large pieces of meat or poultry. Recipe times may vary 20 percent or more, depending on these factors. Cooking times in recipes and charts are only suggestions arrived at under controlled test conditions.

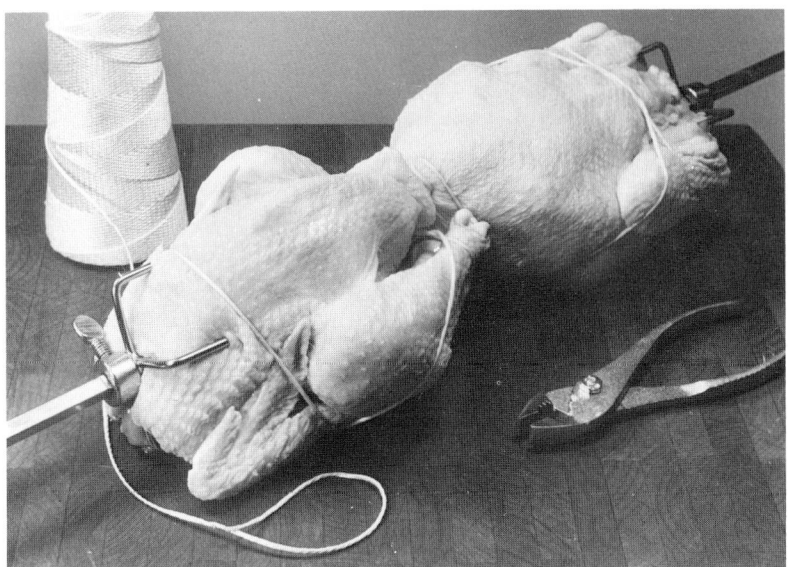

(Above) Two chickens may be skewered and trussed on a single spit. Be sure to tighten the tines securely with pliers.

Spit-roasted game hens have become a family favorite. Barbecue them along with your vegetables and other items on your menu.

ARMENIAN CHICKEN

Yield: 4 servings
Heat Control: low, lid closed, direct heat

Yogurt and mint give this dish a Near Eastern flavor that is delightful.

- 2 chickens halved
- ⅛ teaspoon dried red chili peppers
- ½ teaspoon peppercorns
- 1 pint yogurt
- ½ teaspoon crushed dried mint leaves

Remove skin from chicken halves. With a sharp knife, make a few slits in the meat to absorb marinade flavors. Grind the chili peppers and peppercorns in a blender or with a mortar and pestle. Combine with the remaining ingredients and blend. Pour over the chickens and let marinate 3 hours or overnight. Place the chicken halves on the grill and cook at low, with the lid closed, for 35 minutes, or until done, turning every 10 minutes.

ORANGE-GINGER GAME HENS

Yield: 4–6 servings
Heat Control: low, lid closed, rotisserie

Spicy and very tasty!

- 3 game hens, halved
- ¼ teaspoon pepper
- ¼ cup olive oil
- 1 6-ounce can orange juice concentrate
- 2 tablespoons soy sauce
- 2 tablespoons fresh ginger
- ⅛ teaspoon hot sauce
- 1 clove garlic, crushed

Sprinkle the hens with pepper. Combine olive oil with all the other ingredients and set aside. Place hen halves on a spit. Cook at low, with the lid closed, for 45 minutes. Brush with the marinade every 10 minutes. Hens are done when meat pulls away from the bone easily.

HERBED ROCK CORNISH HENS

Yield: ¾ cup, sufficient for 2 or 3 hens
Heat Control: low, lid closed, warming shelf

This delicious marinade can be used for chicken and turkey, as well as for Rock Cornish Hens.

- 1 Rock Cornish hen per person
- ¼ cup olive oil or cooking oil
- Juice of 1 lemon
- ¼ cup white wine
- 2 tablespoons minced onion
- 1 clove garlic, minced
- ¼ teaspoon rosemary
- ¼ teaspoon tarragon
- ¼ teaspoon thyme
- ¼ teaspoon pepper

Shake ingredients together in a jar. Marinate hens overnight in a plastic bag, turning several times. Use marinade to baste hens during cooking. Cook on low heat, with lid closed, for 35 minutes, on the warming shelf with a drip pan underneath.

ROCK CORNISH HEN

Yield: 1 serving

Heat Control: low, lid closed, warming shelf

Cornish hens are done when the skin is brown and crispy and the wings move easily.

1 Rock Cornish hen
Lemon juice
1 tablespoon butter
½ clove garlic, crushed
1 teaspoon rosemary

Wash Rock Cornish hen off with lemon juice and pat dry. Melt butter, add crushed garlic and rosemary, and brush onto the hen. Place on the warming shelf on low, with the lid closed, for 50–55 minutes, or until nicely browned.

SASSY CHICKEN LEGS

Yield: 4–6 servings

Heat Control: low, lid closed, direct heat

Chicken legs make a delicious and economical meal!

8 chicken legs with thighs
1 6-ounce can tomato paste
½ cup ketchup
¼ cup brown sugar
½ cup dry white wine
1 tablespoon vinegar
1 tablespoon soy sauce
1 tablespoon prepared mustard
1 tablespoon chopped onion
1 teaspoon prepared barbecue spice mix
1 clove garlic, minced
½ teaspoon pepper
¼ cup olive oil

Wash the chicken legs and blot with a paper towel. Combine the remaining ingredients in a saucepan and bring to a boil. Place the legs on the grill and cook on low, with the lid closed, for 30 minutes, turning frequently. Baste with the sauce during the final 5 minutes of cooking.

TURKEY/CHICKEN PATTIES

Yield: 4 servings

Heat Control: low, lid closed, direct heat

Low in calories, low in cholesterol—delicious!

1 pound ground turkey or chicken
4 tablespoons bread crumbs
2½ tablespoons half-and-half or milk
4 scallions, chopped
Salt and pepper to taste
Melted butter

Mix all ingredients except melted butter. Form into 4 patties, ½ inch thick. Brush 1 side with melted butter. Put butter side down on the grill, on low, with the lid closed, and cook for 7 minutes. Brush the top with melted butter; turn and grill another 7 minutes. The butter does not burn and is needed for added moisture.

Save poultry necks, backs, and giblets. Use them for stock in preparation of soup or gravy. Freeze them a few at a time until enough are on hand to fill a soup kettle. Freeze the broth and use it in barbecue and basting sauces.

Heat and smoke are concentrated when the lid is closed. This greatly improves the flavor; however, covered cooking requires a bit more attention.

Amount of Stuffing for Turkeys

WEIGHT	CUPS OF STUFFING
Under 10 lbs.	5 cups
12 lbs.	9 cups
14 lbs.	10½ cups
16 lbs.	12 cups
20 lbs.	15 cups
22 lbs.	16½ cups
24 lbs.	18 cups

A very flavorful and aromatic trick for seasoning meats and poultry is to wrap the wet wood chips in heavy-duty foil in a cylinderlike shape, leaving the ends open. Place these foil packets directly on the briquets toward the front or the coolest part of your grill.

If meat or poultry is getting too dark on the outside, and the proper temperature has not been reached on the thermometer, raise the barbecue cover to the two-inch position.

ROASTED TURKEY

Yield: ¾–1 pound per person

Heat Control: low (2 burners), lid closed, indirect heat

A good choice when serving a large group!

Large whole turkey (self-basting)—12–20 lbs.
Seasonings: such as freshly ground pepper, sage, salt, etc.
1 large onion, sliced ¼-inch slices
Tops of several celery stalks
Small bunch of fresh parsley

Thaw turkey if frozen. Rinse and pat dry. Sprinkle the cavity of the turkey with seasonings, then add vegetables. Tie wings and legs securely, then cover them with oiled heavy-duty aluminum foil to prevent burning. Uncover the wings and legs for the last half hour of cooking time if needed. The aluminum foil must be oiled to prevent it from sticking to the turkey during cooking. Place the turkey on a roasting rack in a shallow aluminum foil pan, filled with water and placed on grid. Cook at low, with lid closed, for 9½ minutes per pound. Occasionally check the pan to make certain there is water in it. With very large birds, it may be necessary to remove wings from turkey when they are done, as they may char before the rest of the turkey is done.

Juices from the turkey that dripped into the water pan may be used to make gravy. Allow the turkey to stand at least 10 minutes before carving.

STUFFED ROASTED TURKEY

Yield: ¾–1 pound per person

Heat Control: low (2 burners), lid closed, indirect heat

Stuffed turkey is delicious any time of year. No need to serve it only at Thanksgiving!

Whole turkey (self-basting)—12–20 lbs.
Your favorite dressing (see chart for correct amount needed)

Thaw turkey if frozen. Rinse and pat dry. Stuff dressing in the cavity of the turkey, then insert poultry nails or sew with poultry thread to close the cavity. Place the turkey on a roasting rack in a shallow aluminum foil pan, filled with water. Tie wings and legs securely, then place oiled heavy-duty aluminum foil over the entire turkey breast and wings. Remove foil during the last hour of cooking time if needed. Cook on low, with lid closed, for approximately 11½ minutes per pound, turning turkey after 2 hours. Check water pan occasionally to make sure it is filled. With extra-large birds, it may be necessary to remove the wings from the turkey

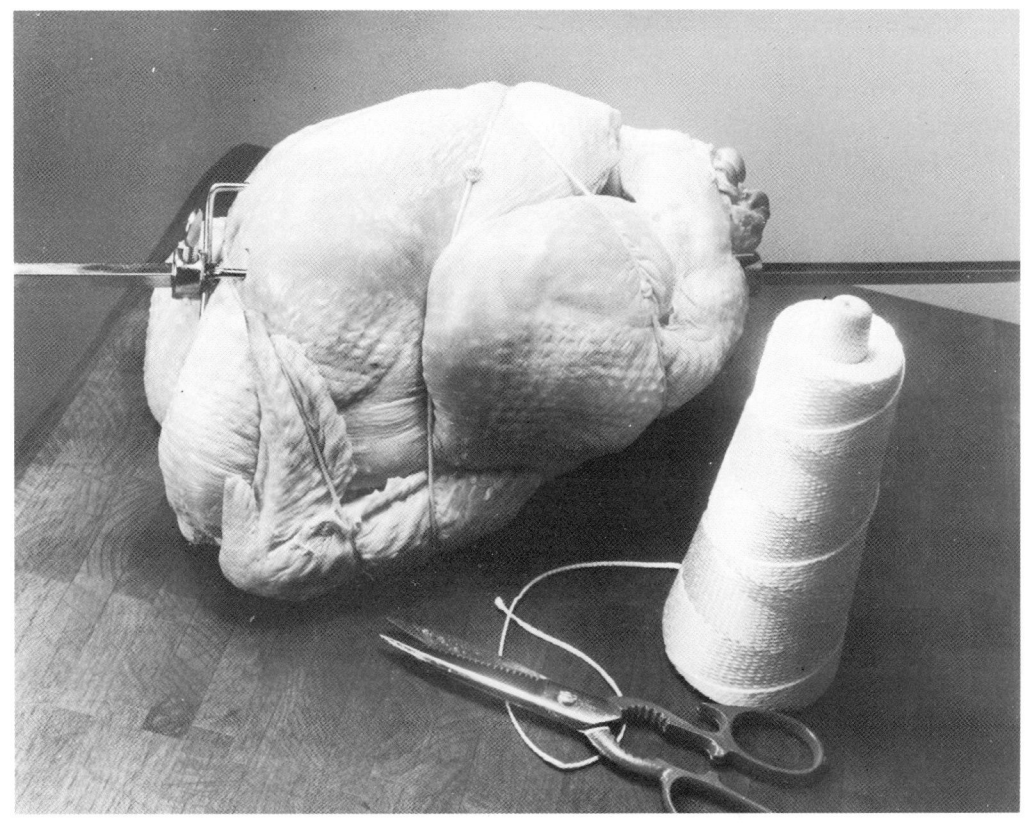

(Left) Whole turkeys must be trussed securely for spit cooking. Check the bird for balance before placing over the heat. Slow cooking ensures a juicy, tender bird.

Tie poultry wings and legs securely before rotisserie cooking. This prevents burning of parts, which may loosen during spit rotation.

For best results and easy carving, allow rotisserie-cooked meats and poultry to stand for a few minutes after cooking.

when they are cooked, as they may char before the rest of turkey is done.

Drippings from the turkey may be used to make gravy. Allow the turkey to stand at least 10 minutes before carving.

SPIT-BARBECUED TURKEY

Yield: 6–8 servings

Heat Control: low, lid closed, rotisserie

This is an easy way to cook a medium-sized turkey.

**1 8–10 lb. turkey, thawed
Sliced onion, celery leaves, and other seasonings, as desired**

Rinse turkey and pat dry. Fill the cavity with sliced onion, celery leaves, and other seasonings, as desired (garlic cloves, bay leaves, peppercorns, and oregano are very good). Truss the turkey with heavy string, tying the legs and tail together and the wings against the breast sides. Close the neck cavity by skewering loose skin into the back with a wooden or metal pick.

Place one holding fork on the spit and insert the spit into the neck cavity, paralleling the backbone. Bring the rod out just above the tail and attach the second holding fork. Push both holding forks securely into the bird and tighten the screws. Check for balance and adjust, if necessary. Be sure the turkey is in the center of the spit rod and secure the holding forks tightly with pliers, if necessary.

Remove the grids from the grill. Attach the spit with the secured and trussed turkey in place. Place a drip pan under the turkey. Remove or push aside the briquets from under the turkey, if needed for clearance. Add water to the drip pan to a depth of 1 inch. Start the rotisserie motor and make sure that the turkey clears the drip pan before igniting the grill. Set the heat on low and close the lid. After two hours, if the wings or legs are browning too much, cover with foil. It is most important to check the water in the drip pan periodically and keep ½–1 inch of water in it to prevent flare-ups. Use a baster when adding more water to the drip pan. This will allow you to refill the drip pan without removing the spit. Check the turkey every 20 minutes, as water evaporates rapidly. A meat thermometer will tell you when the turkey is done. An 8-pound turkey takes approximately 3 hours.

Note: Larger turkeys are best done via indirect cooking on a roasting rack.

Always check rotisserie-cooked foods for balance before placing them on a barbecue.

Fish and Seafood

6

Fish and seafood are probably the most delicate foods that you will be cooking on your gas grill. It's not difficult to cook them; it just requires a little extra attention and careful handling because of the short cooking times and delicate texture.

Outdoor enthusiasts long have bragged that an outdoor fire is the only way to cook fresh fish. Certainly grilled salmon and trout cooked on a grill are classic American favorites. In many ways a modern gas-fired Charmglow barbecue is a big improvement over the open fire. With perfect heat control, fish and shellfish can be cooked exactly the right time and at the right temperature for perfect flavor and texture.

The addition of complementary marinades and basting sauces elevates simple fish cookery to gourmet caliber. Cooking seafood at low heat with the lid down, adding flavoring with wines, herbs, or wood chips, is a culinary accomplishment few fine restaurants can match.

Small whole fish, fillets, steaks, and seafood kabobs are best when quick-grilled or prepared in a rotisserie basket. Whole fish and fillets can also be grilled in a rotisserie basket, which ensures against breakage and eliminates turning. Very small or delicate pieces of fish may also be grilled on a sheet of foil or in a foil pan for easy handling. Use nonstick vegetable spray.

Fish comes in two types, fat and lean (see Fish Chart). You can sometimes tell the difference by feeling the meat. Fat fish may be cooked with a minimum of basting. A little wine or lemon juice should be used during cooking. Lean fish will dry out easily. A basting sauce containing oil or butter, plus seasonings and wine or lemon juice,

(Right) *FOIL LOOPS FOR FISH* (1). Tear off a 12-inch sheet of heavy duty foil. Fold in half lengthwise four times to make a strip 3/4-inch wide. Grease one side of strip and place under fish. (2). Fold in half with ends meeting above the fish. Fold ends together in locked folds until snug against fish. (3). Twist once to secure loop and form handle for turning. (4). To cook fish on the grill, turn fish over with cooking mitts using loop handles. (Use one loop for fish steaks and two for large fish.)

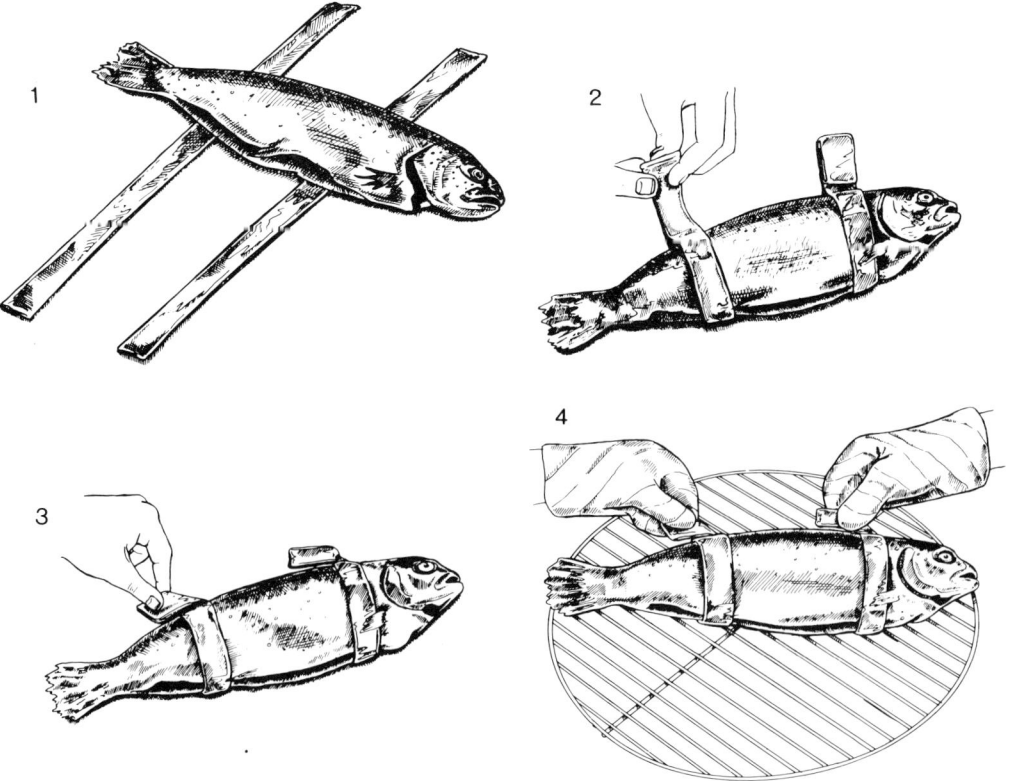

is necessary to provide moisture.

All seafood is done when the flesh turns from translucent to white or opaque. Fish meat will flake easily with a fork when cooked, and shellfish will feel firm when touched. *Overcooking is the greatest danger in fish and seafood cookery.* Follow suggested cooking times carefully, and the results should be rewarding.

Some shellfish, such as crab, lobster, and some shrimp, are sold precooked. This is generally apparent because the shells have turned red or pink. They require only reheating on the barbecue. Overcooking will make them tough and tasteless.

Live lobster and crab should be killed and split or dressed before barbecue cooking. For a barbecue-steamer recipe, they may be dropped into the pot while still alive, just as at the beach. Clams and oysters may be steamed in a pot or cooked right on the grill in their shells.

Freshness is the secret to great seafood cooking, and frozen seafood should always be thawed before cooking.

Fish Chart

The following table shows which fish are fat and which lean.

NAME	FAT	LEAN
Barracuda	X	
Bass, Black Sea		X
Bass, Striped	X	
Bass, California	X	
Bass, White		X
Bass, Rock (also called Black Sea Bass)		X
Black Drum		X
Blackfish		X
Bluefish	X	
Bluegill		X
Bonito	X	
Carp		X
Catfish (5.2% fat-borderline)	X	
Cavalla (also called Jack Crevalle, King Mackerel)	X	
Cobia	X	
Codfish		X
Croaker	X	X
Dab (See Lemon Sole)		

NAME	FAT	LEAN
Drumfish (if referring to a Croaker, both fat and lean)		X
Eel	X	
Finnan Haddie		X
Flounder		X
Fluke (a Flounder is often called a Fluke)		X
Frostfish	X	
Grayling	X	
Grindle		X
Grouper		X
Grunt	X	
Guacamaia		X
Haddock		X
Hake		X
Halfbeak		X
Halibut (4.3% fat-borderline)		X
Herring		X
Kingfish (also called King Mackerel, Fat Fish)	X	X

NAME	FAT	LEAN	NAME	FAT	LEAN
Lemon Sole		X	Snapper, Red		X
Lote	X		Snapper, Blue (also called Bluefish)	X	
Mackerel	X				
Mariposa	X		Sole (also called Flounder)		X
Marlin		X			
Mullet	X		Sucker		X
Muskellunge		X	Sunfish		X
Perch		X	Sturgeon	X	
Pickerel		X	Swordfish		X
Pike		X	Tilefish		X
Pollock		X	Trout (Lake—11.1% fat, Rainbow—6.8% fat, Sea Trout also called Weakfish, Spotted Sea Trout, Speckled Sea Trout, and Spotted Weakfish—3.8% fat)	X	
Pompano (also called Permit)	X				
Porgies		X			
Redfish (also called Channel Bass, Red Bass, Sea Bass)		X			
Salmon	X				
Sardines	X				X
Scrod		X	Tuna or Tunny	X	
Sea Catfish	X		Turbot, Greenland		X
Shad	X		Weakfish (also called Sea Trout)		X
Shark	X	X			
Sheepshead		X	Whale	X	
Shellfish			Whitebait		X
Skate	X		Whitefish	X	
Smelts		X	Whiting		X

NOTE: Generally "fat" fish contain 5-15% oil whereas "lean" fish contain .5-5% oil (mainly concentrated in the liver). *Submitted by Florida Department of Natural Resources.*

BARBECUED SWORDFISH

Yield: 4–6 servings

Heat Control: low, lid closed, direct heat or rotisserie basket

Swordfish is a fatty fish and needs only lemon juice.

2–3 pounds swordfish fillets or steaks
2–3 tablespoons lemon juice

Place fish in a shallow pan. Sprinkle with lemon juice on both sides. Marinate in refrigerator for ½ hour. Secure fish in a rotisserie basket and cook on low, with the lid closed, for 15 minutes or directly on the grill for 8 minutes (4 minutes per side). Fish is done when it flakes easily with a fork.

TROUT WITH CRAB STUFFING

Yield: 6–12 servings

Heat Control: low, lid closed, direct heat

A gourmet treat for a special occasion, this is quite rich, you may wish to split a trout between two diners, depending on appetites and other food served.

1 onion, chopped
2 tablespoons butter
1 cup chopped celery
¼ cup chopped parsley
1 tablespoon drained capers
½ teaspoon salt
⅛ teaspoon pepper
½ cup breadcrumbs
3 tablespoons vermouth
1 pound crabmeat, flaked
6 large trout, cleaned

Combine all ingredients except trout in a mixing bowl, stirring until thoroughly blended. Rinse trout well under cold running water and pat dry. Brush trout inside and out with basting sauce (below). Spoon stuffing into trout and secure cavity with metal skewers. (If you don't have metal skewers, poke holes into trout skin, which is very tough, with a heavy darning needle and use long wooden skewers.) Place trout directly on heat. Cook on low, with the lid closed, for 8 minutes (4 minutes on each side), basting often with basting sauce.

Basting Sauce:

Yield: about ¼ cup

⅛ teaspoon salt
2 tablespoons olive oil
1 tablespoon dry white wine
1 tablespoon lemon juice

Mix sauce ingredients and baste fish with mixture.

Soak wooden skewers in water for an hour before threading fish and grilling.

(Below) Delicate seafood such as whole trout and fillets are best barbecued in a rotisserie basket. Be sure to load the basket loosely so that heat may circulate evenly around the food. Be sure to baste the fish while cooking to retain moisture. Don't overcook!

FISH FILLETS IN LEMON BUTTER

Yield: 6 servings

Heat Control: low, lid closed, indirect heat

A classic seafood recipe adapted for the gas grill.

¼ cup butter, melted
¼ cup dry vermouth
¼ cup lemon juice
1 tablespoon parsley, chopped
6 fish fillets, 1 inch thick (halibut or scrod)
Salt and pepper

Combine butter, vermouth, lemon juice, and parsley and pour over fish fillets. Marinate 30 minutes. Cook in an aluminum foil pan on low, with the lid closed, for 3 minutes, turn, and continue cooking an additional 3 minutes. Cook until the fish flakes easily with a fork, brushing frequently with the marinade. (Thinner fillets will take less cooking time.) Season with salt and pepper just before serving. Pour any remaining marinade over the fish.

JAPANESE BROILED HALIBUT

Yield: 6 servings

Heat Control: low, lid closed, direct heat (1 burner) or rotisserie basket (2 burners)

Oriental seasonings give halibut a very nice, yet different, flavor.

6 halibut steaks, ¼ inch thick (or use swordfish steaks)
2 tablespoons sherry
2 tablespoons lemon juice
½ cup soy sauce
1 teaspoon sugar
¼ teaspoon powdered ginger

Place the halibut steaks in a shallow pan. Combine the remaining ingredients and pour over fish. Marinate at least 1 hour, turning occasionally. Drain marinade and reserve. Place fish on grill or in a rotisserie basket and cook on low (one burner), with the lid closed, for 8 minutes (15 minutes in the basket with both burners). Brush frequently with the marinade.

CHINESE GRILLED HALIBUT

Yield: 6 servings

Heat Control: low, lid closed, direct heat (1 burner) or rotisserie basket (2 burners)

Oriental seasonings give halibut a very nice, yet different flavor.

(Below) Mix a bit of butter, margarine, or oil with lemon juice for basting lean fish. Plain lemon juice with or without white wine is an ideal basting sauce for fatty fish. For a stronger lemon flavor, you may wish to marinate the fillets for 15–20 minutes before grilling.

¼ teaspoon salt
¼ teaspoon pepper
⅛ teaspoon garlic powder
½ teaspoon ground ginger
2 tablespoons cooking oil
3 tablespoons lemon juice
1 teaspoon soy sauce
1½ pounds halibut steaks

Combine all ingredients except fish and mix well. Brush steaks with this seasoning sauce. Place the halibut on the grill and cook on low (1 burner), with the lid closed, for 10 minutes, turning once. Brush frequently with the sauce. You can also use your rotisserie basket for these, placing up to 4 steaks in the rotisserie basket. When using your rotisserie basket, cook for approximately 15 minutes, with 2 burners on low, and the lid closed.

GRILLED SALMON PATTIES
Yield: 4 servings
Heat Control: low, lid closed, direct heat

A budget stretcher that is bound to become a family favorite!

1 15½-ounce can salmon, drained
4 green onions, chopped, with tops
¾ cup crushed crackers
2 eggs, beaten
1 tablespoon chopped parsley
1 tablespoon flour
1 teaspoon salt
¼ teaspoon pepper
Melted butter

Combine all ingredients except butter and shape into 4 patties, about ½ inch thick. Brush the patties generously with melted butter. Place on the grill and cook on low, with the lid closed, for 5 minutes on each side, brushing with butter while cooking.

GRILLED SALMON WITH TARRAGON MAYONNAISE
Yield: 6 servings
Heat Control: low, lid closed, indirect heat

This herb-flavored mayonnaise really complements grilled salmon.

6 salmon steaks, about ½ pound each, cut 1 inch thick
Vegetable oil

Tarragon Mayonnaise
(makes about 1½ cups)
1 cup mayonnaise
¼ cup chopped fresh tarragon or ¼ cup chopped fresh parsley and 2 teaspoons dried tarragon, crumbled
3 tablespoons finely chopped green or red onion
2 tablespoons fresh lemon juice
2 tablespoons chopped capers
¼ teaspoon freshly ground pepper
Salt (optional)
Lemon wedges for garnish

Brush salmon steaks with oil and arrange on an oiled pan for grilling. Combine the Tarragon Mayonnaise ingredients in a bowl or food processor until well blended. This can be done a day in advance, if desired. Chill at least 2 hours before using. You may wish to sprinkle a little lemon juice over the salmon steaks before grilling in the pan. Grill for approximately 12 minutes on low, with the lid closed, turning once. Serve with Tarragon Mayonnaise.

GRILLED SALMON

Yield: 4 servings

Heat Control: low, lid closed, indirect heat or rotisserie basket

This is a gas grill adaptation from Scandinavia, where cooks are famous for their salmon recipes.

4 salmon steaks, about ½ pound each, 1 inch thick
Oil (preferably olive oil)
Freshly ground pepper to taste
2 large cloves garlic
1 tablespoon dried dill
Juice of 1 lemon

Wipe fish dry. Brush both sides with oil, then season on both sides with pepper. Arrange in an aluminum foil pan or a rotisserie basket. Crush the garlic cloves by hitting them with the back of a heavy spoon, and rub the salmon surfaces with the garlic. Sprinkle with dill and ½ the lemon juice. Place on a preheated grill or use the basket and cook on low, with the lid closed, about 10 minutes, basting occasionally with natural juices. Sprinkle with the remaining lemon juice and serve immediately.

Fish is a very delicate meat. Care should be taken not to overcook it.

The Charmglow is slanted to help drain excess dripping to the rear of the fire box. This feature helps control heat and aids in preventing possible flare-ups.

SHANGHAI GRILLED RED SNAPPER

Yield: 6 servings

Heat Control: low, lid closed, indirect heat

Cooking red snapper in foil with this sauce keeps it very moist.

¼ teaspoon pepper
⅛ teaspoon garlic powder
½ teaspoon ground ginger
3 tablespoons cooking oil
3 tablespoons lemon juice
1 tablespoon soy sauce
1½ pounds red snapper fillet

Combine all ingredients except fish and mix well. Place red snapper in an aluminum foil pan in a single layer and cook on low, with the lid closed, for 3 minutes per side, brushing frequently with the sauce.

FOIL-WRAPPED FISH

Yield: 6 servings

Heat Control: low, lid closed, indirect heat

If your meal is casual, you may wish to serve this fish in the foil packets. For more formal occasions, transfer it to individual heated serving plates.

6 whole small freshwater pan fish, about 9 ounces each
¼ pound butter, melted
Salt and pepper
Juice of 2 or 3 lemons
Parsley

Brush cleaned fish inside and out with butter and sprinkle with salt and pepper. Tear off squares of heavy-duty aluminum foil that are large enough to wrap an individual fish.

Spray foil with nonstick vegetable spray and center fish on it. Close the foil packets and secure the edges tightly. Place on preheated grill. Cook at low for 15 minutes, with the lid closed, or until the fish flakes with a fork. Open the foil to let in barbecue smoke during the final 5 minutes. Sprinkle with lemon juice. Serve garnished with parsley and remaining melted butter.

Fish and Seafood

RAINBOW TROUT

Yield: 4–6 servings

Heat Control: low, lid closed, direct heat or rotisserie basket

Salad dressing gives trout a tangy flavor.

4–6 whole rainbow trout, about 13 oz. each
1   8-ounce bottle Italian salad dressing

Wash the trout inside and out and blot dry with a paper towel. Marinate in dressing for 3 hours or overnight. This can be done in a covered dish or a plastic bag. If dressing does not cover trout entirely, turn several times.

Use heavy-duty aluminum foil with several holes poked into it. Spray with nonstick vegetable spray and arrange the trout on the foil. Cook for a total of 12 minutes over low heat, with the lid closed, turning once.

To cook in a rotisserie basket, allow a few extra minutes of cooking time.

Marinate shrimp in soy sauce for 10 minutes, turning frequently. Mix butter and lemon juice. Thread shrimp on wooden skewers that have been soaked in water for an hour or more and place on a preheated grill. Cook on low, with the lid closed, for 6 minutes, basting with the lemon butter. Turn and broil about 3 minutes longer. Transfer shrimp from the grill to a hot platter and pour remaining lemon butter over shrimp. Sprinkle with freshly chopped parsley.

(Above) Many foods may be barbecued directly in foil. Vegetables may be wrapped in double-thick pouches and cooked right on the grill. Fish fillets and whole trout may also be sealed in foil envelopes and cooked on the grill. Be sure not to puncture the foil when turning. Use tongs or a wide spatula.

ORIENTAL SHRIMP ON A SKEWER

Yield: 6–8 servings

Heat Control: low, lid closed, direct heat

You'll love the smoky barbecue flavor of these shrimp.

3   pounds large shrimp, shelled and cleaned
½ cup soy sauce
½ cup butter or margarine, melted
¼ cup lemon juice
3   tablespoons chopped parsley

Variations: Other shellfish such as prawns, crayfish, and lobster tails can be used instead of shrimp. Medium-sized lobster tails (about 8 ounces each) should be grilled, shell side down, for 6 minutes. Turn and grill an additional 4 minutes.

Peeled prawns should be grilled 6 minutes on one side and 4 minutes on the other. Peeled crayfish, which are smaller, should be grilled 3 minutes on one side, 2 on the other.

SHRIMP AND MUSHROOM BROCHETTE

Yield: 2–3 servings

Heat Control: low, lid closed, direct heat

Serve these delectable shrimp over parsleyed or fried rice.

- ⅓ cup champagne vinegar or white wine vinegar
- Juice of 1 lemon
- ¼ cup soy sauce
- ⅓ cup cooking oil
- ¼ teaspoon salt
- 1 clove garlic, crushed
- ⅛ teaspoon powdered ginger
- 1 teaspoon sugar
- 1 pound fresh shrimp
- ½ pound fresh mushrooms

Combine vinegar, lemon juice, soy sauce, oil, salt, garlic, ginger, and sugar in a deep bowl. Shell and devein shrimp. Wash mushrooms and remove stems. Add shrimp and mushrooms to marinade. Let stand several hours in the refrigerator. Thread shrimp and mushrooms on skewers. Place on the grill and cook on low, with the lid closed, for 8 minutes, turning frequently with a spatula rather than tongs.

Although fresh lemon juice is preferred, it is not always available. The juice of one lemon equals three tablespoons. Frozen lemon juice is a better substitute than the reconstituted lemon juice.

LEMON SCAMPI

Yield: 4–6 servings

Heat Control: low (1 burner), lid closed, indirect heat

The delicate lemon and garlic flavor of this treat will delight everyone.

- 2 pounds jumbo shrimp
- ¼ pound butter
- 1 teaspoon salt
- ⅛ teaspoon red pepper sauce
- 1 clove garlic, minced
- 1 tablespoon chopped parsley
- Juice of 1 lemon

Clean and devein the shrimp, leaving the tails on. Melt the butter and stir in the remaining ingredients. Place the shrimp on a double thickness of foil and pour the seasoning sauce over them. Fold up the foil to form a tightly closed envelope. Place the packet directly on the grill. Cook on low, over indirect heat, with the lid closed, for 5 minutes, or until steam escapes from the packet. Remove the packet from the grill immediately and transfer shrimp to warmed serving platter. Pour the cooking juices over the shrimp and serve or serve the sauce separately as a table sauce.

SCALLOPS IN SHELLS

Yield: 6-8 servings

Heat Control: low, lid closed, indirect heat

Serving scallops in these shells is easy as well as attractive.

- 6 scallop baking shells (or shell-shaped foil cups)
- Melted butter
- 2 pounds fresh sea or bay scallops
- Juice of 1 lemon
- 4 tablespoons melted butter or margarine
- 2 tablespoons white wine
- Salt and pepper
- ¼ cup chopped parsley
- 1 green onion, minced

Brush the inside of the shells with butter. Rinse the scallops and divide them among 6-8 individual serving shells. (Usually ⅓ pound per person is ample; for smaller portions, serve ¼ pound per person.) Sprinkle with lemon juice. Blend the remaining ingredients and spoon over the scallops. Wrap each shell in a double thickness of heavy-duty foil and place on a preheated grill, shell side down. Cook on low, with the lid closed, for 30 minutes, opening the package at the top during the final 5 minutes. If scallops seem too dry, pour in additional melted butter or wine. Scallops are done when firm and sauce is steaming hot.

If you don't have any serving shells, scallops can also be prepared in an aluminum foil pan. Cover with foil and cook for 15–20 minutes.

NEW ENGLAND CLAM BAKE

Yield: 4 servings

Heat Control: low, lid closed, pot directly on briquets

A fantastic informal meal. Serve with a tossed salad and hot French bread.

- 1 pound fresh clams in shell, any variety
- ½ pound lobster tails, cut up
- ½ pound king crab legs, cut up
- ½ pound scallops
- 2 tablespoons butter or margarine
- 1 bay leaf
- 1 clove garlic, crushed
- ½ cup dry white wine
- ½ cup water
- ½ teaspoon salt
- 2 tablespoons chopped green onion
- ¼ teaspoon Tabasco sauce

Combine all ingredients in a heavy kettle, such as a cast-aluminum dutch oven or a cast-iron pot. Be sure the bay leaf is immersed in the liquid. Place the covered kettle directly on the briquets and cook on low, using two burners, with the lid closed, for 25 minutes. To serve, divide seafood among 4 bowls. Pour broth over and serve with hot French bread to dip into broth.

LOBSTER TAILS ON THE GRILL

Yield: 4 servings

Heat Control: low, lid closed, direct heat

A real treat for special occasions.

- 4 8-ounce lobster tails, cleaned and thawed, if frozen
- 1 stick butter or margarine, melted
- 1 clove garlic, or one shallot, minced
- 1 tablespoon finely chopped parsley
- ¼ cup dry white wine

Cut the lobster tails almost through the membrane on the underside and spread open. This is easily done with kitchen shears or a very sharp knife. Combine the remaining ingredients and spread on the lobster flesh. Place lobster tails on the grill, shell side down. Cook on low, with the lid closed, for 5 minutes, then turn and cook an additional 4 minutes with meat side down. Serve with remaining seasoned butter.

Very fresh ingredients are the secret to successful fish and seafood cooking.

Vegetables and Fruits

7

Most barbecue cooks don't take full advantage of the barbecue in cooking vegetables and fruits. Corn on the cob and foil-wrapped potatoes, of course, are common. But why not Greek-style eggplant and American-style baked apples?

These and many more delightful vegetable combinations cook to perfection on the grill. A sealed foil pouch or an aluminum foil pan is the secret to many of the recipes. A wok for stir-frying adds still more variety, and crocks for beans and casseroles, as well as a flambé pan for flaming fruits for dessert, can be used with ease.

In most menu planning there is room on the grill or warming shelf for a packet of vegetables. In many cases these accompaniments are enhanced with the aromas from cooking meats. Simply open the packet during the final minutes of cooking so that the vegetables can absorb barbecue and smoke flavors.

Economy and convenience are also barbecue bonuses. Frozen vegetables, as well as fresh ones, cook beautifully on the Charmglow, eliminating any mess in the kitchen.

As with conventional cooking, do not overcook vegetables. Check the cooking time on the recipe so that you can start at the proper time to be done at the same time as the rest of the meal.

(Right) *BUNDLE WRAP* (1). Place food in center of a sheet of heavy duty foil large enough to permit adequate wrapping. (2). Bring 4 corners of foil up together in a pyramid shape. (3). Fold the open edges together in a series of locked folds. For cooking, fold loosely to allow for heat circulation and expansion. For freezing, fold until foil is tightly molded and sealed against food.

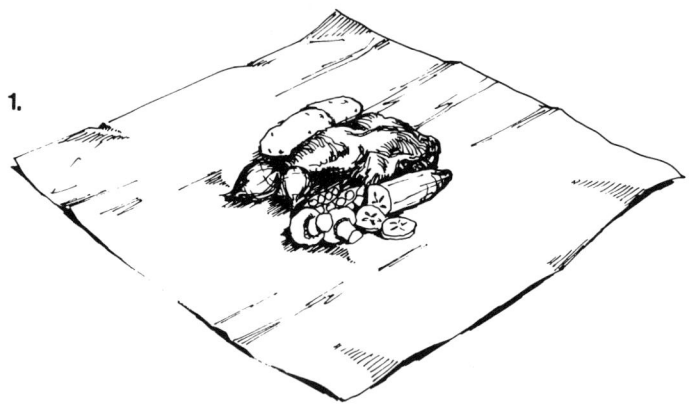

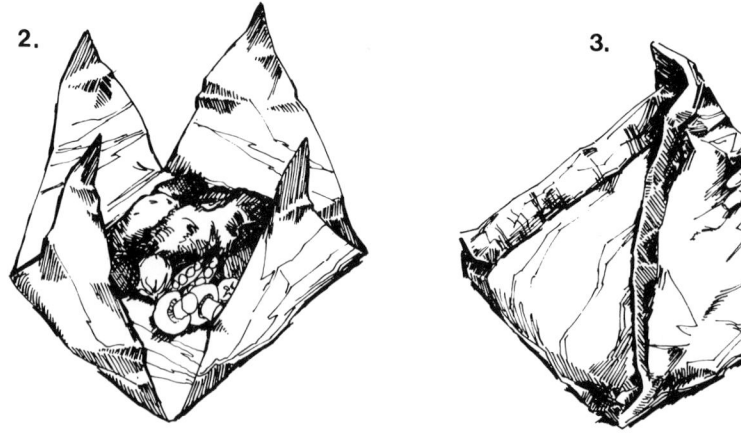

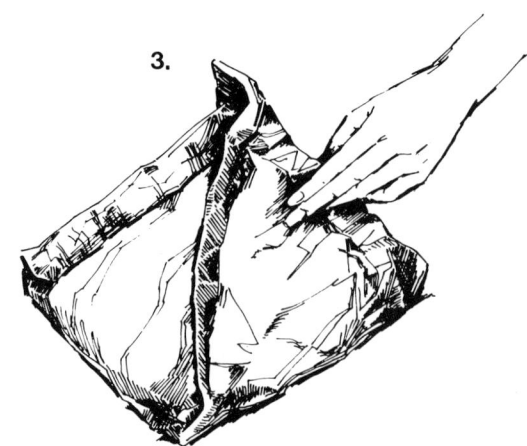

Vegetables and Fruits

GREEN BEANS 'N' MUSHROOMS

Yield: 4 servings

Heat Control: low, lid closed, warming shelf

A longer cooking time makes this a perfect vegetable dish to prepare on grill while a roast or steak is cooking.

- 1 12-ounce package frozen french-cut green beans
- 1 tablespoon butter or margarine
- ¼ cup fresh mushrooms, sliced, or 1 small can sliced mushrooms
- ¼ teaspoon pepper
- 1–2 tablespoons chopped green onion

Combine ingredients and enclose in a double thickness of heavy-duty foil. Place on a warming shelf. Cook on low, with the lid closed, for 35 minutes, turning 2–3 times during cooking. If the beans are thawed, reduce cooking time by 15 minutes.

STEAMED CAULIFLOWER

Yield: 6–8 servings

Heat Control: low, lid closed, warming shelf

This is an easy way to steam cauliflower on your grill.

- 1 large head cauliflower (about 4¾ pounds)
- ¼ cup water
- 1 tablespoon butter (more if desired)
- Salt and pepper to taste

Place the cleaned head of cauliflower on a large piece of heavy-duty aluminum foil. Add butter, water, and salt and pepper and wrap tightly. Set on the warming shelf for about 30 minutes, on low, with the lid closed. (Smaller heads of cauliflower will take less time.)

Variation: Add several pieces of sliced or grated cheddar cheese to the packet during the last 5 minutes of cooking or use Brown Butter Sauce (see recipe).

(Above) Most green vegetables, both fresh and frozen, may be barbecue-cooked in foil. Seasonings such as herbs, wine, butter, and sauces may be combined with the vegetables. Then seal in a pouch for carefree cooking.

BUTTERED BEETS

Yield: 3–4 servings

Heat Control: low, lid open 1 inch, warming shelf

Small, tender, garden-fresh beets are best for this recipe.

- 4 small beets
- 1 tablespoon butter
- 1 tablespoon water

Cut off tops and peel the beets with a potato peeler. Put into a square of heavy-duty foil, dot with butter, and sprinkle with water. Close the packet securely and place on the warming shelf for 20–25 minutes on low, with the lid open 1 inch. Cooking time is the same whether beets are placed all in one packet or in individual packets.

EGGPLANT EL GRECO

Yield: 4 servings

Heat Control: low, lid open 1 inch, indirect heat

A stuffing of celery, onions, olives, feta cheese, and seasonings crowns this unusual eggplant dish.

- 1 large eggplant
- ½ cup Italian-style spiced green or black olives
- 3 stalks celery, finely chopped
- ½ medium red onion, finely chopped
- ½ pound feta or Jack cheese, cut into small cubes
- 3 tablespoons finely chopped green onion tops
- ½ teaspoon pepper
- ½ teaspoon oregano
- 3 tablespoons olive oil

Cut eggplant into lengthwise quarters. With a sharp knife cut out the seedy center of the eggplant quarters, leaving an inch-thick shell; set aside. Dice the eggplant that was removed from the centers and combine it with the remaining ingredients. Prepare 4 14-by-20-inch double-thick aluminum foil sheets. Place scooped-out quarter shells of eggplant in the center of each piece of foil. Fill the shells with the eggplant mixture. Fold foil to form a sealed envelope. Place on the grill. Cook on low for 25 minutes (check the packets after 20 minutes) with the lid open 1 inch.

CHUCK WAGON BEAN POT

Yield: 5–6 servings

Heat Control: low, lid closed, indirect heat

This economical dish is terrific with hamburgers, bratwursts, or ribs.

- 1 28-ounce can baked beans
- 3 tablespoons ketchup
- 3 tablespoons molasses
- 1 teaspoon dry mustard
- ¼ teaspoon prepared barbecue spice mix
- ¼ teaspoon onion salt or onion powder
- 2 slices bacon, cooked and chopped

Mix together all ingredients in a heavy pot or bean pot. Place on the grill. Cook on low, with the lid closed, for 15 minutes. Stir about every 5 minutes, so the beans don't burn on the bottom of the pot.

BOURBON BAKED BEANS

Yield: 12–20 servings

Heat Control: low, lid closed, direct heat

Because this easy recipe serves up to 20 people, it's a favorite for parties.

- 4 16-ounce cans Boston baked beans
- ¾ teaspoon dry mustard
- 1 cup chili sauce
- ½ cup bourbon
- ½ cup strong black coffee
- 1 16-ounce can crushed pineapple, drained
- 4 tablespoons brown sugar

Combine all ingredients in a large, heavy casserole, bean crock, or baking dish, and place on a preheated grill. Cook, uncovered, for 25 minutes on low, with the lid closed, stirring every 10 minutes.

When not in use, keep your barbecue unit covered and protected from weather for long life and reliable operation.

Measure your bean pot to be sure that pot and lid fit under the grill with the lid closed before you heat the grill and fill the bean pot.

Vegetables and Fruits

ZESTY BAKED BEANS

Yield: 16–24 servings
Heat Control: low, lid closed, direct heat

Strips of bacon adorn the top of this classic dish.

4–5 pounds canned pork and beans
½ cup chopped onion
¼ cup chopped celery
⅓ cup chopped green pepper
2 tablespoons prepared mustard
½ cup molasses
1 teaspoon Worcestershire sauce
5 dashes Tabasco sauce
½ cup barbecue sauce
½ cup ketchup
2 strips bacon, uncooked and cut in quarters

Combine all ingredients except bacon in a large ovenproof container. Lay the bacon strips on top. Cook on low, with the lid closed, for 20 minutes. Stir every 10 minutes.

Variation: Add browned ground meat to the beans.

BOSTON BAKED BEANS

Yield: 10–12 servings
Heat Control: low, lid closed, indirect heat

Make these beans in a large pot and serve for family gatherings or parties.

3 1-pound cans (6 cups) pork and beans in tomato sauce
1 tablespoon wine vinegar
1 tablespoon soy sauce
1 tablespoon Worcestershire sauce
¾ cup ketchup
10 slices smoked bacon, cut into small pieces

Empty 1 can of beans into a very large casserole or glazed bean pot. Combine the seasoning ingredients and sprinkle ⅓ of the mixture over the beans. Repeat for the second and third cans of beans. Place the casserole on the grill. Cook on low, with the lid closed, for 15 minutes. Stir once or twice during cooking.

STUFFED ZUCCHINI

Yield: 6 servings (entrée)
      8–12 servings (side dish)
Heat Control: low, lid closed, indirect heat or warming shelf

These stuffed zucchini can be prepared ahead and refrigerated until ready to grill. They are great as a side dish or meatless main course.

6 medium zucchini
½ onion, finely chopped
3 tablespoons melted butter
¾ cup buttered breadcrumbs
2 medium tomatoes, peeled and chopped
2 tablespoons minced parsley
1 cup mozzarella cheese, cut into ½-inch cubes
Salt and pepper to taste

Halve zucchini lengthwise. With the pointed end of a spoon, scoop out the inside and chop finely. Combine the remaining ingredients with the chopped zucchini. Fill the shells with the mixture. Place 2 halves on a large double thickness of aluminum foil that has been brushed with butter. Close the packets securely and place them on the grill. Cook on low, with the lid closed, for 10 minutes, or until done, turning frequently. Or cook for 15 minutes on the warming shelf—no need to turn.

Any basic casserole or baked-dish recipe that requires a 350° F. oven may be cooked on a Charmglow unit with the lid closed, the heat set on low, and one burner. The Charmglow duplicates the conditions in a moderate-heat conventional oven.

ACORN SQUASH WITH APPLES

Yield: 2 servings

Heat Control: low, lid open 1 inch, indirect heat

This nutritious vegetable is especially good with pork and poultry.

- 1 medium-sized acorn squash
- 1 cup diced unpeeled apples
- 2 tablespoons brown sugar
- 1 teaspoon cinnamon
- 2 tablespoons butter or margarine
- ¼ cup chopped pecans or walnuts

Halve squash lengthwise and scoop out the seeds. Combine the remaining ingredients and fill the centers of the squash halves with apples, brown sugar, cinnamon, butter, and nut mixture. Wrap each half securely in heavy-duty aluminum foil. Place on the grill, cut side up, and cook on low with the lid open 1 inch, for about 50 minutes or until done.

Shortcut Cooking: For quicker cooking, cook whole squash in a microwave oven for 8 minutes. Cut in half and follow the above instructions. Cooking time on the grill will be greatly reduced, to about 20 minutes.

MUSHROOMS IN FOIL

Yield: 4 servings

Heat Control: low, lid closed, indirect heat

These are delicious spooned over freshly grilled steak.

- ½ pound fresh mushrooms, whole, halved, or sliced
- 1½ tablespoons butter
- 1 tablespoon sherry (optional)
- 2 tablespoons parsley or other fresh herbs
- 1 teaspoon Worcestershire sauce

Wash and rinse mushrooms well. Place on a sheet of heavy-duty aluminum foil. Dot with butter and seasonings. Wrap edges securely. Place on the grill and cook on low, with the lid closed, for 12 minutes, turning the packet every 5 minutes.

ASPARAGUS WITH LEMON BUTTER

Yield: 4 servings

Heat Control: low, lid closed, indirect heat

These delicious crisp vegetables can be made with fresh or frozen asparagus.

- 1 pound fresh asparagus or 1 10-ounce package frozen asparagus spears
- 3 tablespoons butter
- 2 tablespoons lemon juice
- Salt and pepper to taste

For fresh asparagus, wash thoroughly and break off tough ends. Arrange the spears on foil, top with remaining ingredients, seal packet, and cook on low, with the lid closed, for 15–20 minutes, depending on the size of the asparagus. Place frozen asparagus on heavy-duty foil, cut large enough to fold. Put the remaining ingredients over the asparagus. Seal and place the packet on the grill. Cook on low for 30 minutes, with the lid closed. If asparagus is thawed, reduce cooking time to 15 minutes.

Shiny and dull sides of aluminum foil work in the same way. You can shield or make packages with either side out. In the manufacturing process two pieces of aluminum foil are rolled out together. The sides that touch the rollers become shiny; the other sides, not in direct contact with the rollers, have a matte finish.

Vegetables and Fruits

BASTED GARDEN VEGETABLES

Yield: about 1½ cups
Heat Control: low, lid closed, direct heat

A delicious and low-calorie way to prepare your garden-fresh vegetables. Most of the oil in the marinade will cook off, leaving a delectable blend of flavors minus the calories.

Juice of 2 lemons
1 medium onion, sliced
1 bay leaf
½ cup white wine
½ cup olive oil
6 peppercorns

Combine ingredients in a saucepan and cook slowly over moderate heat for 10 minutes. Remove from heat and cool.

Thread vegetables such as cauliflower, green peppers, small onions, mushrooms, zucchini, and eggplant on skewers. Brush generously with sauce and cook on low, turning skewers every 3–4 minutes, depending on the vegetables used. Tomatoes do not work well on skewers, they tend to become soft and fall off skewers before other vegetables are cooked.

FRESH GRILLED TOMATOES

Yield: 6 servings
Heat Control: low, lid closed, indirect heat or warming shelf

Tomato halves may be wrapped individually or in one large package of aluminum foil, whichever is more convenient for serving.

3 large, firm tomatoes
1 tablespoon plus 1 teaspoon melted butter or margarine
1½ teaspoons garlic salt
2 tablespoons grated Parmesan cheese, Italian breadcrumbs, or a combination of both
4 teaspoons chopped parsley

Wash and halve tomatoes. Place cut side up on double-thick aluminum foil. Brush the tomatoes with melted butter or margarine. Sprinkle about ¼ teaspoon of garlic salt and 1 teaspoon of Parmesan cheese (or breadcrumbs) over tomatoes. Top with parsley. Wrap foil loosely over the tomatoes and place on the grill. Cook on low with the lid closed, for 10 minutes or on the warming shelf for 17 minutes.

DILLED CARROTS

Yield: about 4 servings (depending on size of carrots)
Heat Control: low, lid closed, indirect heat

These carrots will go well with just about anything.

8 tender young carrots
1 tablespoon butter or margarine
½ teaspoon dried dill weed
Dash water

Wash and scrape carrots. Place carrots on double thickness of heavy-duty aluminum foil, or use a small aluminum foil pan. Dot with butter or margarine. Sprinkle with dill and water. Wrap in foil or cover pan securely with foil. Cook on the grill on low, with the lid closed, for 50–55 minutes, or until fork-tender, turning frequently.

Variation: Substitute an herb of your choice for the dill.

Vegetables to be cooked in foil should be cut into equal-sized pieces for uniform cooking.

Weather may be a factor in heat selection. On cold or windy days increased cooking time may be required.

Heavy-duty aluminum foil is the barbecue chef's best friend. Experiment by shielding delicate foods and wrapping corn and potatoes. Foil often eliminates any kitchen cleanup afterward.

CORN ROASTED IN THE HUSK

Heat Control: low, lid closed, direct heat

Roasting corn this way gives it a very different flavor than boiled or steamed corn. Many people prefer it, but it involves a good deal more work to prepare.

Choose corn that has none of the husk removed. Peel back the husk and remove all the silk. Carefully rewrap the husks around the corn and tie the ends together with string or wire twists. Soak in water for at least half an hour, preferably longer. Roast on the grill over low heat, with the lid closed, for 15–20 minutes. Turn at least 2 or 3 times. Serve with lots of butter, salt, and pepper.

CORN IN FOIL

Yield: 3–6 servings (1–2 ears per person)
Heat Control: low, lid closed, indirect heat

When fresh corn is in season and is at its best, you may wish to plan for two or more ears per person, depending on the other food being served and the heartiness of appetites.

4–6 ears young tender sweet corn
Butter or margarine, softened
Lemon pepper or seasoned salt

Strip off the corn husks and remove the silk. Brush the corn with softened butter or margarine and generously season with lemon pepper or seasoned salt. Lay each ear on a double thickness of aluminum foil. Sprinkle with a little water and wrap the foil securely around the corn. Place the corn on the grill and cook on low for about 15 minutes, with the lid closed. (For very tender baby corn, 10 minutes should be sufficient.) Turn every 5 minutes.

Variations: Garlic salt and/or other herbs may be used. Several ears of corn may be placed in 1 foil packet.

ONION KISSES

Yield: 1 serving
Heat Control: low, lid closed, warming shelf

Try to select a sweet onion for this recipe. This dish may be prepared ahead.

1	**medium onion**
1	**teaspoon instant beef bouillon granules or 1 cube beef bouillon**

Take 1 medium onion, peel, and trim the top of the onion. Place in a 9-by-9-inch piece of heavy-duty aluminum foil. Sprinkle with bouillon granules. Twist the top of the foil like a chocolate kiss, place on the warming shelf, and cook on low, with the lid closed, for about 25 minutes, or until onion is tender.

BAKED POTATOES

Yield: 4 servings
Heat Control: low, lid closed, indirect heat

Basic information for baking potatoes on your gas grill.

4	**medium-sized Idaho potatoes (see note below)**

Butter or margarine
Salt and pepper to taste
Sour cream or yogurt (optional)
Chives (optional)

Scrub potatoes and pat dry. Wrap each potato in a double

thickness of aluminum foil. Place the potatoes on the grill and cook on low, with the lid closed, for 25–35 minutes (see cooking chart below), turning every 5 minutes, until the potatoes are soft. To serve, open the foil and break the skin with a fork. Dot with butter or margarine and season with salt and pepper. Top with sour cream or yogurt, and sprinkle with snipped chives, if desired.

Potato Cooking Chart

Size	Time
Small	25 minutes
Medium	30 minutes
Large	35 minutes

Note: Idaho potatoes are not always available. Russet potatoes are also good, but they may take 5–10 minutes longer to cook. For crisp skins, open the foil packets during the final 10 minutes of cooking.

POTATOES BAKED IN FOIL WITH BACON AND CHEESE

Yield: 4 servings

Heat Control: *low, lid closed, direct heat*

Foil makes a casserole dish for these layered potatoes.

6   slices bacon
1   pound cheddar or American cheese
1   large onion
4   medium-sized baking potatoes
2   tablespoons butter
¼   cup chopped chives (optional)

Cook the bacon until crisp, and blot well with a paper towel; crumble. Cut cheese and onions into small cubes, or slice or grate with a food processor. Peel and slice the potatoes ¼ inch thick. Grease or spray with nonstick vegetable spray an 8-by-8-inch aluminum foil pan. Place a layer of potatoes in the bottom of the pan, then sprinkle a layer of cheese and onions on top; repeat the layers until all the ingredients are used. Dot with butter. Sprinkle with chives, if desired. Seal tightly in the foil. Place over direct heat on your grill, on low, with the lid closed, and bake until the potatoes are done, about 35–40 minutes, depending on the thickness of the potato slices.

IRISH POTATOES

Yield: 6 servings

Heat Control: *low, lid closed, direct heat or warming shelf*

These potatoes are nicely browned and need no additional seasonings.

6   medium potatoes
1   green pepper, diced
1   onion, chopped
    Seasoned salt
¼   cup melted butter

Peel the potatoes and cut into lengthwise quarters. Place each potato on a 14-inch square of heavy-duty aluminum foil and sprinkle with diced pepper, onion, and seasoned salt. Fold up the edges and pour the butter equally over the potatoes. Seal the foil and place on the grill. Cook on low, with the lid closed, for 17 minutes. You may also use the warming shelf, on low, for 22 minutes. (The size of the potatoes used will influence the cooking time.) Turn the potatoes several times. Serve in foil packets.

Because of the many variables such as wind, outdoor temperature, and grill models, always check foil packets every 5 minutes during the last 10–15 minutes of cooking.

When vegetables, fruits, and other foods are to be cooked without a barbecue flavor, seal them in tightly closed foil pouches and cook on the grill. When a smoke or a barbecue flavor is desired, leave the foil packets partially opened to allow smoke to permeate the food or open them toward the end of the cooking period.

The selection of complementary vegetables and fruits is as important to a barbecue menu as the meat.

SPICED APPLES

Yield: 4 to 6 servings

Heat Control: low, lid closed, direct or warming shelf

These apples may be served as a side dish or a dessert. They may be cooked on the edge of the grill or the warming shelf, whichever is more convenient.

**4 to 6 large baking apples
½ cup brown sugar, maple syrup, or honey
¼ cup butter, melted
½ teaspoon cinnamon and mace (optional)
½ cup raisins (optional)
Whipped cream or vanilla ice cream**

Wash and core apples. Place each on a double thickness of heavy-duty foil. Combine remaining ingredients and fill the centers of the apples with this mixture. Close edges of foil securely. Place the foil packages on the grill. Cook on low for 35 minutes, with lid closed (smaller apples will take 25-30 minutes). Allow 45 minutes if placed on the warming shelf. Apples are done when soft. Serve topped with whipped cream or a scoop of vanilla ice cream, if using grilled apples for a dessert. These apples make an excellent garnish for pork.

GRILLED PEARS

Yield: 1 serving

Heat Control: low (1 burner), lid closed, indirect heat

A delight for calorie watchers, because no sugar is added to this dessert.

**½ fresh Bosc or Anjou pear
Lemon juice
Cinnamon
Ginger**

Sprinkle each pear half lightly with lemon juice, cinnamon, and ginger. Wrap carefully in heavy-duty aluminum foil and grill on low over indirect heat, with the lid closed, for 45 minutes.

BANANAS FLAMBÉ

Yield: 6 servings

Heat Control: low, lid open, direct heat

This flaming dessert is a neat and fun way to end a patio meal.

**4 bananas
6 tablespoons butter
4 tablespoons brown sugar
¼ teaspoon cinnamon (optional)
Dash nutmeg
¼ cup brandy
¼ cup banana liqueur
Vanilla or chocolate ice cream**

Slice the bananas ¼ inch thick and set aside. In a shallow skillet or flambé pan, melt the butter and add the brown sugar. Continue cooking on low, with the lid open, until the sugar becomes caramelized, add bananas, and stir, coating them for a few minutes. Add the brandy and banana liqueur and continue stirring until the mixture becomes well blended. Flame and serve over vanilla or chocolate ice cream.

To flame outdoors can be a little bit difficult in gusty weather. It is best to add some pure-proof alcohol to your brandy for flaming purposes. Because of wind and other conditions, this is probably the only way to flame outside with certainty.

Variation: You may wish to add ¼ teaspoon of cinnamon and a dash of nutmeg. If you like your bananas on the soft side, you can sauté them in the butter and then add the sugar and continue cooking to caramelize.

Hamburgers, Hot Dogs, Sandwiches, and Breads

8

Barbecue sandwiches needn't be limited to hamburgers and hot dogs. Succulent roast beef, Italian sausage, and steak sandwiches deserve party status. Grilled combinations of seasoned meat and cheese can satisfy any hearty appetite.

Many sandwich recipes may be prepared well in advance and refrigerated or frozen prior to grill cooking. Wrapped in foil, they may then be tossed onto the Charmglow grill and heated to order.

Use your Charmglow as a party sandwich buffet server. Hot sliced meats may be sauced and kept warm on low, with only one burner on. Let guests toast buns on the grill and build their own sandwiches. Many sandwiches, such as Reuben Dogs, Hot Tuna Sandwiches, Shrimp Buns, Hot Ham 'n Cheese Burgers, and other combination sandwiches, may be wrapped in foil and held for several hours on low heat on the warming rack for backyard and informal group snacks.

Hot barbecued breads offer the Charmglow owner a wide variety of tastes. Aromatic cheese and garlic-seasoned French breads are traditional, but adding a pinch of herbs and exotic spices can surprise guests.

Some bread recipes double as main dishes. Selecting a complementary hot bread or roll recipe is as important as choosing the meat— and a must on any traditional American barbecue menu.

BASIC GRILLED HAMBURGERS

Grilled hamburger patties are best made with a high grade of beef with between 15 and 20 percent fat content. If the fat content is lower, the grilled burgers tend to be dry, and if the fat content is higher, you will be plagued with flare-up problems caused by excessive dripping of grease into your grill. Mix your ingredients together as quickly as possible; the less they are handled, the more tender, tasty, and juicy they'll be. Have patties at room temperature before grilling.

Brats with extremely high fat content may cause flare-ups.

Sausage Cooking Chart

BRATWURST *		
Fresh	Low/lid closed	8 min.
Smoked	Low/lid closed	6 min.
HOT DOGS*	Low/lid closed	4 min.
ITALIAN SAUSAGE*	Low/lid closed	22 min.
KNOCKWURST*	Low/lid closed	6 min.
POLISH SAUSAGE*	Low/lid closed	6 min.
SMOKED SAUSAGE*	Low/lid closed	20 min.
TURKEY OR CHICKEN DOGS*	(same as Hot Dogs)	

*Turn several times

Add salt after grilling for juicier patties.

Hamburger Cooking Chart
The following chart is intended for ¼-pound hamburger patties (3½ inches across and 1 inch thick), cooked on low, with the lid open, over direct heat. (Thinner patties will cook more quickly.)

> Rare—2–2½ minutes on each side
> Medium-rare—2½ minutes on each side
> Medium—3 minutes on each side
> Well-done—4 minutes on each side

Variations To 1½ pounds of ground beef, add any of the following ingredients.
- 1 teaspoon oregano
- ¼ cup chopped parsley
- ⅓ cup chopped dill pickles
- ⅓ cup pickle relish
- ½ cup cheddar, American, or blue cheese
- 1 teaspoon chili powder
- ¼ cup chili sauce or ketchup
- 1 tablespoon Worcestershire sauce or steak sauce
- ¼ cup toasted sesame seeds
- ¼ cup tomato juice
- ¼ cup sour cream or yogurt
- ¼ cup dry red wine
- 1 tablespoon dry minced onion

No barbecue experience is complete without traditional hot dogs and hamburgers. Chargrilling ensures juicy and flavorful results every time, at home or on a picnic.

Heat in your gas grill is more intense toward the back of the grill. If you are going to grill hamburger patties to various stages of doneness, put those that you want cooked more thoroughly toward the rear and those you want on the rarer side toward the front. In this fashion you may cook all your hamburger patties simultaneously.

BACON BURGERS

Yield: 4 servings

Heat Control: low, lid closed, direct heat

Bacon, cheeses, and other seasonings dress up these burgers.

- 4 slices bacon, cooked and crumbled
- 1½ pounds ground beef
- ½ cup dry red wine
- 1 tablespoon chopped parsley
- 1 teaspoon Worcestershire sauce
- ½ cup grated cheddar cheese
- ¼ teaspoon pepper

Combine all ingredients and form into 6 patties. Cook on low, with the lid closed, as indicated under Basic Grilled Burgers (see recipe).

DELUXE CHEESEBURGERS

Yield: 4–6 servings

Heat Control: low, lid closed, direct heat

These cheeseburgers are made extra moist with tomato juice.

- 1½ pounds ground beef
- ½ teaspoon celery seed
- ⅛ teaspoon pepper
- ½ cup tomato juice
- ⅔ cup chopped stuffed green olives
- 3 tablespoons chopped fresh parsley
- 2 tablespoons chopped onion
- 6 slices American cheese

Mix all ingredients except cheese; shape into 6 patties. Place on the grill and cook on low, with the lid closed, as indicated in Basic Grilled Burgers (see chart). Just before removing the patties from grill, place a slice of cheese on each patty and continue cooking until the cheese melts, usually another minute.

MUSHROOM BURGERS

Yield: 4–6 servings (¼ pound for each patty)

Heat Control: low, lid closed, direct heat

The mushrooms cook in the beef fat, giving them a sautéed flavor.

- 1½ pounds ground beef
- ⅛ teaspoon pepper (optional)
- 12 large fresh mushrooms or 1 6-ounce can mushrooms, coarsley chopped or sliced
- Parsley for garnish

Lightly mix all ingredients and shape into 6 patties. Place on the grill and cook on low, with the lid closed, for 2 minutes on each side (medium-rare). Garnish with sprigs of parsley.

STEVE'S HAMBURGERS

Yield: 5 ¼-pound patties

Heat Control: low, lid closed, direct heat

No need to salt these hamburgers, because chopped green olives give them plenty of zest.

- 1 pound chopped sirloin
- ¼ cup chopped onions
- ½ cup finely chopped pimiento-stuffed green olives
- 1 cup cubed or grated Colby or cheddar cheese

Combine all the ingredients and shape into 5 equal-sized patties. Grill on low, with the lid closed, for 4 minutes on each side (medium-rare).

DEVILED HAMBURGER ON FRENCH BREAD

Yield: 4 servings

Heat Control: low, lid closed, direct heat

Cut into small pieces, this recipe can also be used as an appetizer.

- 1 **pound lean ground beef or ground chuck**
- 2½ **teaspoons Worcestershire sauce**
- 3 **tablespoons frozen chopped onions**
- 2½ **teaspoons prepared mustard**
- 1 **pound loaf of French bread**

Combine all of the above ingredients and spread on French bread which has been cut lengthwise. Grill meat side down on low, with the lid closed for 15 minutes. Watch carefully, because these loaves char easily. Remove from heat and slice crosswise to serve.

MEXICAN BURGERS

Yield: 6 patties

Heat Control: low, lid closed, direct heat

For a more intense Mexican spiciness, increase the amount of chili powder and cumin in these burgers.

- 1½ **pounds ground beef**
- ⅛ **teaspoon pepper**
- ¼ **cup grated Monterey Jack or American cheese**
- ¼ **cup tomato juice**
- 1 **teaspoon chili powder**
- ¼ **teaspoon cumin**

Lightly mix ingredients and shape into 6 patties. Place on the grill and cook as indicated in Basic Grilled Burgers (see recipe).

BEST HAMBURGER EVER

Yield: 4 servings

Heat Control: low, lid closed, direct heat

No need for buns here. Serve these just as you would a steak, with sauce over the meat.

- 4 **large mushrooms**
- 4 **tablespoons butter**
- 4 **scallions, including tender part of green, chopped**
- 2 **pounds ground chuck**
- 1 **tablespoon good strong mustard**
- **Few drops Worcestershire sauce**
- **Freshly ground pepper**
- 3 **tablespoons chopped parsley**
- ⅓ **cup dry red wine**
- **Salt to taste**

Separate the mushroom caps from the stems and coarsely chop the stems. Sauté mushrooms in 1 tablespoon of the butter until just cooked through, about 5 minutes. Remove with a slotted spoon and set aside. In the same skillet, gently sauté the scallions in the remaining butter until limp. Meanwhile, put the ground meat into a bowl. Add the mustard and Worcestershire sauce and season with salt and pepper. Add the scallions and most of the butter they were cooked in, leaving only a thin film of fat in the skillet. Toss 2 tablespoons of the parsley into the meat and mix gently with your fingers. Shape into 4 large hamburgers, keeping meat light, never slapping it down. Place on the grill and cook on low for 2 minutes on each side, with the lid closed. Remove hamburgers. Combine wine with sautéed mushrooms in the skillet and cook to heat through. This can be done on the grill. Pour over the grilled patties. Sprinkle with the remaining parsley. Salt to taste.

Use the low setting for most grilled meats, steaks, chops, and hamburgers.

Always have meats, poultry, and seafood at room temperature before cooking. Foods taken directly from the refrigerator to the grill will require longer cooking. Most frozen foods require thawing. Very thin steaks and hamburger patties may be placed on the grill frozen.

STROGANOFF BURGERS

Yield: 4–6 ¼-pound patties
Heat Control: low, lid closed, direct heat

The sour cream or yogurt gives these burgers a moist and creamy flavor.

1½ pounds ground beef
⅛ teaspoon pepper (optional)
¼ cup commercial sour cream or yogurt
1 tablespoon minced parsley
¼ teaspoon garlic salt

Lightly mix all ingredients and shape into 6 patties. Place on the grill and cook on low, with the lid closed, for 2 minutes on each side (medium-rare). Serve on thinly sliced toasted Russian rye bread.

Variation: Add ½ cup chopped green peppers or ¼ pound chopped or sliced mushrooms to the meat mixture.

ORIENTAL BURGERS

Yield: 4–6 servings
Heat Control: low, lid closed, direct heat

Serve these burgers with sprouts instead of lettuce for a nice change.

1½ pounds ground beef
⅛ teaspoon pepper (optional)
¼ cup dry sherry
2 tablespoons fresh mushrooms, chopped
¼ teaspoon ground ginger
1 tablespoon soy sauce

Lightly mix all ingredients and shape into 6 patties. Place on the grill and cook on low, with the lid closed, for 2 minutes on each side (medium-rare). Serve with hot rice and stir-fried Oriental vegetables.

ALL-AMERICAN HOT DOG

Yield: 4–6 servings
Heat Control: low, lid closed, direct heat

You can have a meal ready in five minutes cooking these on your gas grill.

6 hot dogs
6 hot dog buns
Butter

Place hot dogs on the grill and cook on low, with the lid closed, for 2 minutes per side, turning with tongs. During the last minute, place split and buttered buns face down on the grill to toast. Slip browned hot dogs into buns and serve with any combination of pickle relish, mustard, ketchup, onions, chopped tomatoes, and shredded lettuce.

Variation: Wrap hot dogs with partially cooked bacon strips and secure with toothpicks.

CHEDDAR DOGS

Yield: 8 servings
Heat Control: low, lid closed, warming shelf

These can be prepared in advance and then cooked on the grill at the last minute.

8 wieners, each cut into 9–10 round slices
½ cup grated sharp cheddar cheese
2 hard-cooked eggs, chopped
4 tablespoons chili sauce
2 tablespoons pickle relish
1 teaspoon prepared mustard
½ teaspoon garlic salt
8 hot dog buns, sliced opened

Scrape out the inside of the bun tops and bottoms with a fork, leaving the crusts intact. (Toast the crumbs and use as a bread topping for vegetables or other casseroles.) Combine the remaining ingredients and heap the mixture into the buns. Cover with the tops and wrap each dog in aluminum foil. Cook on the warming shelf for 10 minutes, with your grill set on low and the lid closed.

REUBEN DOGS

Yield: 6 servings
Heat Control: low, lid closed, direct heat

Less expensive than the famous Reuben sandwich, but just as tasty.

6 hot dogs
6 hot dog buns
Mustard
1 8-ounce can sauerkraut, well drained
2 tablespoons Thousand Island dressing
¼ pound sliced Swiss cheese
Kosher dill pickle slices or slivers

Place the hot dogs on the grill and cook on low, with the lid closed, for about 2 minutes on each side, or until heated through, turning frequently. Slice the hot dogs down the center and place each one in the center of a hot dog bun. Spread the center of each hot dog with a little mustard. Add ⅙ of the sauerkraut topped with 1 teaspoon of Thousand Island dressing. Cover with Swiss cheese and place the top on the bun. Wrap in heavy-duty aluminum foil or put into a foil pan and return to grill until the cheese is melted and bubbly, about 5 minutes. Garnish with dill pickle slices or slivers and serve immediately.

GRILLED GERMAN BRATWICHES

Yield: 4 servings
Heat Control: low, lid closed, direct heat

Seasoned onions and cheese enhance these bratwurst sausages.

4 smoked bratwurst links (about 12 ounces)
1½ cups coarsely chopped onion
1½ cups (1 12-ounce can) beer
2 tablespoons butter or margarine, softened
½ teaspoon onion salt
4 hot dog buns
½ cup (2 ounces) shredded sharp natural cheddar cheese

Brown the bratwurst on low heat on the grill, with the lid closed, for approximately 6 minutes, turning often. Combine onion, beer, and grilled brats in a saucepan and simmer, uncovered, for 20–30 minutes, on the grill (may also be done indoors). Stir together the butter or margarine and the onion salt; spread on the buns. Place buttered buns on the grill for a minute, buttered side down, to toast. Remove the brats from the beer and make a lengthwise slit in each to within ½ inch of the ends. Fill with cheese and place in the buns with cheese side up. Place each in a foil pan. Return to the grill and heat for 2 minutes or until cheese melts. Fresh bratwurst can also be used but will take approximately 8 minutes to grill, 4 minutes per side.

Because the high setting on your LP Gas Grill produces such intense heat, regular grilling should not be done on this setting.

Any foods cooked at medium require frequent turning and constant attention.

BRATS IN BEER WISCONSIN-STYLE

Yield: 4–8 servings (1–1½ brats per person, depending on accompaniments)

Heat Control: low, lid closed, direct heat

The key to this traditional recipe is to soak the brats periodically in beer.

6–8 fresh bratwurst links
1   12-ounce can or bottle beer
½ cup chopped onions

Combine the beer with ½ cup chopped onions in a pan and bring to a boil; lower heat to simmer, add uncooked brats, and cook for about 10 minutes. This can be done right on the grill. Heat the grill and brown the brats on low, with the lid closed, for 5 minutes, turning frequently. When the brats are done, serve on toasted buns or with potato salad and beans. If you wish, you can place the brats in beer for a few minutes halfway through cooking, then return to grill and continue cooking until done.

ITALIAN SAUSAGE (MILD OR HOT)

Yield: ½ pound per person

Heat Control: low, lid closed, direct heat

Use these sausages as an accompaniment to a pasta dish or for delicious sandwiches.

Italian sausage links
Tomato Sauce (see recipe)

Place the sausages on the grids over low heat, with the lid closed, and cook slowly, turning the sausages frequently, for approximately 22 minutes. (Cooking them on medium will cause excessive flare-ups, which would dry out your sausages.) Serve with Tomato Sauce.

KRAUT-AND-BACON-STUFFED BARBECUED SAUSAGES

Yield: 8 servings (about 24 appetizers)

Heat Control: low, lid open and closed, rotisserie basket

Surprise your guests with this most attractive and tasty treat. Cut into 1-inch pieces, they make marvelous hors d'oeuvres.

10 slices bacon
2   large smoked sausages, about 1 pound each
1   8-ounce can sauerkraut, drained and chopped
¼   cup chili sauce
2   tablespoons chopped onion
1   teaspoon brown sugar
1   teaspoon caraway seeds

Partly cook the bacon (in a pan on your grill or stove), drain, and set aside. Slit the sausages lengthwise almost to the ends but only ¾ of the way through. Hollow out the center of each sausage with a sharp pointed teaspoon, making sure that you leave the shell intact. Mix the scooped-out meat with the sauerkraut and the remaining ingredients. Stuff the mixture into the slit in each sausage and wrap each with 5 bacon slices, using wooden picks to secure the bacon. Put the sausages into a rotisserie basket and grill on low with the lid propped open, for 10 minutes; then close the lid and continue cooking for another 10 minutes.

PITA BREAD STUFFED WITH LAMB

Yield: 6 servings
Heat Control: low, lid closed, direct heat

A fantastic Near Eastern treat.

1¼ pound boned shoulder or leg of lamb, thinly sliced
6 pitas
Butter
⅓ cup lemon juice
⅛ teaspoon salt
⅛ teaspoon freshly ground pepper
½ bay leaf
1 small clove garlic, crushed
½ teaspoon oregano
Garnish: shredded lettuce, tomato wedges, green pepper slices, onion slices
½ cup sour cream

For ease in preparation, have the butcher slice the lamb for you. Combine the lemon juice, salt, pepper, bay leaf, garlic, and oregano and mix well. Marinate the lamb slices in this sauce for 30 minutes. Trim excess fat from the lamb. Cook the lamb on the grill, turned low with the lid closed, for 10 minutes, turning once. Cut pita bread in half through the center and put several meat slices into each pocket. Lightly butter the outside of the pita loaves. Wrap them in foil and put them on the grill for 8 minutes on low, with lid closed. Garnish with vegetables as desired and spoon sour cream over the top. Serve immediately.

SOURDOUGH MEAT LOAF

Yield: 6 hearty servings
Heat Control: low, lid open 1 inch, warming shelf

This meat loaf is quite literally a savory meat mixture packed into a hollowed-out bread loaf.

1 long 15-ounce loaf sourdough bread (preferably with rounded, not pointed, ends)
¾ cup sour cream or yogurt, or ½ of each
2 eggs
1½ pounds very lean ground beef
½ cup shredded cheddar cheese
¼ cup dry red wine
½ green pepper, finely chopped
3 whole green onions, finely chopped
1 tablespoon chopped fresh parsley
1 teaspoon Worcestershire sauce
½ teaspoon seasoned salt
½ teaspoon pepper
2 tablespoons melted butter

With a very sharp knife, cut a thin lengthwise slice from the top of the bread loaf. Reserve this lid. With your fingers, scoop out as much of the crumb from the bread as possible. Shred enough of this bread to make 1½ firmly packed cups of crumbs. Set aside. In a large mixing bowl, combine the remaining ingredients except the butter with the reserved breadcrumbs. Fill the hollowed-out loaf with the meat mixture, packing it in firmly. The meat mixture should be level with the top of the loaf. If there is any extra meat mixture, barbecue it in separate patties. Top the loaf with the lid and brush the entire outside crust with melted butter. Place the loaf on a double thickness of foil and wrap tightly. Place it on the warming shelf and cook on low, with the lid open 1 inch, for 45 minutes, turning often. Test the meat in the center to see if it's done. Let cool 10 minutes for better slicing.

Shiny or dull sides of aluminum foil work in the same way. You can shield or make packages with either side out. In the manufacturing process, two pieces of aluminum foil are rolled out together. The sides that touch the rollers become shiny; the other sides, not in direct contact with the rollers, have a matte finish.

HOT SWISS BACON SANDWICH LOAF

Yield: 1 1-pound loaf

Heat Control: low, lid closed, indirect heat (1 burner) or warming shelf

Use as a luncheon entrée, a tasty snack, or cut into quarters and serve as hors d'oeuvres.

- 1 cup (2 sticks) butter or margarine
- 2 tablespoons freshly snipped or freeze-dried chives
- Grated rind of 1 lemon
- 1 tablespoon lemon juice
- ¼ teaspoon freshly ground pepper
- 1 tablespoon Dijon mustard
- 2 teaspoons poppy seeds
- 1 1-pound loaf bakery sandwich bread, sliced
- 16 ounces Swiss cheese, sliced thin
- ½ pound bacon, cooked crisp, drained and crumbled (see note below)

In a mixing bowl or a food processor, cream the butter or margarine until light and fluffy. Add chives, lemon rind, lemon juice, pepper, mustard, and poppy seeds. Continue mixing until thoroughly blended. Set aside 2 tablespoons of this mixture and spread the remainder on all cut surfaces of the bread. In between every other cut slice, place 1 slice of Swiss cheese, sprinkle with crumbled bacon, and stack. Continue until all the bread slices have been assembled. Spread remaining lemon-butter mixture on the top and sides of the loaf. Cover with foil and bake on low (1 burner) over indirect heat or on the warming shelf for 12–15 minutes.

Note: Bacon can be fried in a skillet or cooked in a microwave oven for approximately 1 minute per strip. Another way is to oven-fry bacon. Lay bacon on top of your broiling pan in a single layer and put into a preheated 400° F. oven. Bake for 8–10 minutes, depending on how crisp you want it. (This timing is for thin-sliced bacon; thicker slices will take longer.) There's no need to turn the bacon; it stays flat and there seems to be much less shrinkage when bacon is cooked in this manner. When removing grease from bacon on paper towels, use an extra towel to blot the top. (This works well for anything greasy that you're trying to drain.)

NACHO SANDWICHES

Yield: 1 sandwich

Heat Control: low, lid closed, indirect heat

These make a very simple yet nutritious luncheon or snack, to be cooked on your patio or by your pool.

- 1 tablespoon (or less) butter or margarine
- 2 slices white or wheat bread
- 1 thin slice Monterey Jack cheese
- 1 thin slice mozzarella cheese
- 1 thin slice cheddar cheese
- Mild or hot chilies

Spread butter or margarine on one side of each slice of bread. With buttered sides out, sandwich the cheese slices, topped with chilies, between the slices of bread. Place the sandwich on an aluminum foil pan and grill on low, with the lid closed, for 5 minutes on each side. The bread should be lightly toasted on each side and the cheese melted inside. Cut the sandwich in half and serve.

HOT HAM 'N CHEESE BURGERS

Yield: 8 generous burgers
Heat Control: low, lid closed, warming shelf

This is a great way to use leftover ham and a nice change from traditional beef hamburgers. Make the filling, fill the buns, and wrap them in foil in advance. Then simply put them on your grill. Presto—your meal is ready! These are ideal for teenage parties, late night snacks, and weekend lunches and suppers.

- 1 cup ground ham
- 1 cup grated or shredded cheddar cheese
- ¼ cup sweet relish or chopped dill pickles
- ¼ cup mayonnaise
- 8 hamburger buns

Combine all the ingredients except buns in a bowl. Generously fill hamburger buns, place in an aluminum foil pan, and cover with foil, or wrap buns individually. Bake on the warming shelf over low heat, with the lid closed, for 20–25 minutes.

SHRIMP BUNS

Yield: 4–6 servings
Heat Control: low, lid closed, direct heat

A good make-ahead recipe—guests can heat their own when ready.

- 1 4¼-ounce can shrimp, cut into pieces
- 2 hard-cooked eggs
- 1 apple, finely chopped
- ¼ cup chopped green pepper
- ¼ cup chopped celery
- ¼ cup chopped lettuce
- 1–2 tablespoons mayonnaise
- Salt and pepper to taste
- Sliced American or cheddar cheese
- Hamburger buns

Blend all ingredients except cheese and buns, using enough mayonnaise to moisten the mixture. Season with salt and pepper. Spread the mixture on halves of buns and top each with a slice of cheese and top of bun. Place in an aluminum foil pan and put on the grill. Heat on low, with the lid closed, for 6 minutes. The sandwiches should be heated through and the cheese melted.

HOT TUNA SANDWICHES

Yield: 9 sandwiches
Heat Control: low, lid closed, warming shelf

This is marvelous for a crowd because it can be made in advance and frozen, then thawed at room temperature before heating on the grill.

- ¼ pound shredded or grated cheddar cheese
- 1 6½-ounce can tuna
- ¼ cup mayonnaise
- ¼ cup sour cream or yogurt
- 1 2¼-ounce can chopped or sliced ripe olives
- 2 tablespoons chopped onions
- 2 tablespoons chopped green pepper
- 2 tablespoons sweet relish
- 9 hamburger buns

Combine all ingredients except buns. Generously fill buns and place in an aluminum pan and cover with foil or wrap buns individually. Bake on the warming shelf over low heat for 20 minutes, or until heated through, with the lid closed.

SWISS TUNA GRILL

Yield: 8 servings
Heat Control: low, lid closed, direct heat

These grilled sandwiches are nutritious and quick to make.

- 1 6½-ounce can tuna, drained and flaked
- ½ cup (2 ounces) shredded process Swiss cheese
- ½ cup chopped celery
- 2 tablespoons finely chopped onion
- ¼ cup mayonnaise or salad dressing
- ¼ cup dairy sour cream or yogurt
- Dash pepper
- 16 slices rye bread
- Butter or margarine, softened

Combine tuna, cheese, celery, onion, mayonnaise, sour cream or yogurt, and pepper. Spread filling on 8 bread slices. Top with remaining bread slices. Spread the outside of the sandwiches with softened butter or margarine. Place in an aluminum foil pan and place on the grill. Cook on low, with the lid closed, for 3 minutes on each side, or until the filling is heated through and both sides of the bread are toasted.

STROGANOFF STEAK SANDWICH

Yield: 6 sandwiches on French hero-sized rolls, 12 servings on sliced French bread
Heat Control: low, lid closed, direct heat

This recipe is as pleasing to the eye as it is easy to prepare.

- ⅔ cup beer
- ⅓ cup cooking oil
- 1 teaspoon salt
- ¼ teaspoon garlic powder
- ¼ teaspoon pepper
- 2 pounds flank steak, about 1 inch thick
- 2 tablespoons butter or margarine
- ½ teaspoon paprika
- Dash salt
- 4 cups sliced Spanish onions
- 12 slices French bread, toasted, or 6 hero-sized French rolls, halved lengthwise and toasted
- 1 cup dairy sour cream or yogurt, warmed
- ½ teaspoon prepared horseradish
- Paprika for garnish (optional)

In a shallow dish, combine the beer, oil, 1 teaspoon salt, garlic powder, and pepper. Place the flank steak in the marinade and cover. Marinate overnight in the refrigerator or several hours at room temperature; drain. Grill on direct heat on low, with the lid closed, for 8 minutes per side (medium-rare), turning several times. In a flame-proof saucepan, melt the butter or margarine by putting it on the grill while the meat is cooking. Blend in paprika and a dash of salt. Add the onion and cook until tender but not brown. Thinly slice the meat on the diagonal across the grain. For each serving, arrange the meat slices over French bread or rolls. Top with onions. Combine the sour cream or yogurt and the horseradish; spoon onto each sandwich. Sprinkle with paprika, if desired. Serve open-faced.

ITALIAN STEAK SANDWICH

Yield: 6 large sandwiches
Heat Control: low, lid closed, direct heat

Salt causes the natural juices of meat to flow out. For juicier meat, always salt after grilling.

These steak sandwiches are terrific for parties. Grill meat and assemble the sandwiches in advance and then, at serving time, just heat through until the cheese is melted.

6 sandwich steaks
6 onion rolls
1 large Spanish onion, sliced
1 large green pepper, coarsely chopped
1 large tomato, coarsely chopped
½ cup Italian salad dressing
1 6-ounce package sliced mozzarella cheese

Combine the onion, green pepper, and tomato in the salad dressing and marinate for ½ hour or longer. While the vegetables are marinating, quickly sear the steaks on the grill on low, with the lid closed, for 2 minutes on each side. Cut the rolls in half (you may toast the cut side of the rolls for a minute) and place a steak on each roll. After the vegetables have marinated, sauté with the marinade in a skillet on the grill for a few minutes until they are soft. Divide the vegetables among the sandwich steaks and top with a slice of cheese. Add the top of the roll and wrap in foil. When ready to serve, heat the rolls on low with the lid closed, for 2 minutes on each side.

FLANK STEAK AND CHEESE SANDWICHES

Yield: 6–8 servings

Heat Control: high and then low to finish, lid open, direct heat

Cooking the flank steak initially on high heat and then lowering the temperature seems to have a tenderizing effect on the meat.

2 flank steaks, scored
Garlic salt
Pepper
6 onion rolls or French rolls, buttered
1 10-ounce crock sharp cheddar cheese spread, at room temperature
2 red onions, chopped fine

Several hours before barbecuing, score the meat and sprinkle the steaks with garlic salt and pepper. Grill the steaks on high for 5 minutes (2½ minutes per side), then on low for 3 minutes (1½ minutes per side) or until medium-rare, with the lid open. Remove the steaks and place the buns on the grill cut side down. Cook until slightly toasted. Slice the steak on the diagonal, against the grain, in very thin slices. Place 5 or 6 slices on the bottom half of each bun. If necessary, trim the slices so that they do not hang over the buns. Spread cheese on the top half of each bun and sprinkle red onion on the meat. Serve immediately.

BROWN-AND-SERVE ROLLS ON A SPIT

Yield: 1 dozen rolls

Heat Control: low, lid closed, indirect heat

Really a fun, delicious, and very different way of making brown-and-serve rolls.

Brown-and-serve rolls
Melted butter

Thread brown-and-serve rolls on a spit and brush with melted butter. Cook on low, with the lid closed, for 5 minutes, or until the rolls are brown on all sides.

The high setting should be used only for quick searing of meats to be cooked rare.

Aluminum foil pans make ideal cookware for refrigerator biscuits, brownie mix, brown-and-serve sausages, and many other convenience foods.

(Above) To obtain a crisp surface on seasoned grilled French bread, place loaf crusts back to back and wrap securely in foil. Bread may now be grilled on both sides with the seasoned side facing the heat.

mixture continually with a pastry brush, because the salad dressing mix tends to settle at the bottom. Divide the bread into family-sized servings and wrap in heavy-duty foil. Heat the foil-wrapped loaf on the warming shelf, on low, with the lid closed, for 20 minutes. If the garlic bread is frozen, thaw at room temperature for about an hour before heating on the grill. Open the foil-wrapped loaf and check to see that it's heated all the way through before serving.

GARLIC BREAD

Yield: 1 1-pound loaf

Heat Control: low, lid closed, warming shelf

While you're at it, it's just as easy to prepare several loaves of garlic bread and freeze the extra loaves for future meals. You'll be glad you did. A loaf of garlic bread will turn the simplest meal into a festive occasion. For an extra flavor treat, sprinkle parmesan cheese on buttered slices before wrapping in foil. Serve with a salad on a warm summer evening.

¼ **pound butter or margarine**
½ **package dry garlic-and-cheese salad dressing mix**
1 **long, thin 1-pound loaf French or Italian bread**

Melt the butter or margarine. (In this recipe margarine tastes every bit as good as butter.) Add the salad dressing mix. Meanwhile, using a bread knife, cut the bread into diagonal slices, 1 to 1½ inches thick, making sure not to cut through the bottom crust, so that the loaf will remain intact. With a pastry brush, liberally brush the butter and garlic mixture on the sliced surfaces. Stir the butter

FROZEN BREAD

Yield: 1 medium-sized loaf

Heat Control: low, lid closed, warming shelf

Everybody loves the taste and smell of warm baked bread. Your grill will bake these loaves beautifully—a delicious accompaniment to many grilled meals.

1 **loaf frozen white baking dough**

Follow the package instructions for thawing the dough and for the rising. Be sure to use an aluminum bread pan that is at least 8½ by 4½ by 2½ inches, or your bread will rise too high and possibly touch the top of your grill. When the bread is ready to be baked, place the pan on the warming shelf of your grill, set the temperature on low, with the lid closed, and bake for 30 minutes. Your bread should be nicely browned and crispy on top. Remove from the grill and place on a cutting board. Let the bread rest for 5 minutes before slicing with a bread knife. Be sure to have on hand an ample amount of butter to complement this marvelous treat.

ROQUEFORT BREAD

Yield: 6–8 servings
Heat Control: low, lid closed, warming shelf

Blue cheese lovers will adore this. It goes particularly well with beef.

- ¼ pound (1 stick) butter or margarine, softened
- ⅛ pound Roquefort or Blue cheese, at room temperature
- 1 tablespoon fresh chives or thawed frozen chives
- 1 large loaf unsliced French bread

Combine butter, cheese, and chives. Cut the bread into slices and spread the butter mixture on one side of each slice. Place the slices together and wrap the bread in foil. Place the bread on the warming shelf, turning several times. Cook on low, with the lid closed, for 12 minutes.

ONION-CHEESE LOAF

Yield: 6–8 servings
Heat Control: low (1 burner), lid closed, warming shelf

Butter, mustard, cheese, and onions distinguish this loaf from the mundane.

- 1 thin, long 1-pound loaf French or Italian bread
- ¼ pound butter or margarine
- 3 tablespoons prepared mustard
- 1 8-ounce package sharp American cheese or cheddar cheese
- 1 small Spanish onion, cut into thin slices

Cut bread diagonally at 1-inch intervals, cutting to but not through the bottom crust. Blend the butter or margarine with prepared mustard; spread over cut surfaces. Insert a slice or ½ a slice of cheese and a thin slice of onion into each slash. Wrap the loaf in heavy-duty foil and place on the warming shelf. Heat on low (1 burner), with the lid closed, for 15 minutes, turning once after 7 minutes, or until heated through and the cheese melts.

CHEESE-STUFFED FRENCH ROLLS

Yield: 12 rolls
Heat Control: low, lid closed, warming shelf

This recipe can be the feature of a meatless meal.

- 12 large French rolls
- ½ pound cheddar cheese, grated
- 1 tablespoon mayonnaise
- 1 8-ounce can tomato sauce
- 4 green onions, chopped
- 1 7-ounce can ripe olives, chopped
- 2 hard-cooked eggs, chopped
- Salt and pepper to taste
- 1 4-ounce can green chilies, chopped
- 2 tablespoons vinegar
- 2 cloves garlic, crushed

Remove some bread from the center of each roll. Combine the remaining ingredients (use a food processor if you have one). Divide the mixture equally among the 12 rolls. Replace the top of the rolls, wrap each in aluminum foil, and place on the grill. Cook on the warming shelf for 5 minutes on low, with the lid closed.

When heating bread and other items on the warming shelf, both burners are probably on and you are probably grilling other foods at the same time. If, however, that isn't the case, use one burner and increase the cooking time by five minutes.

REFRIGERATED BISCUITS

Heat Control: low, lid closed, warming shelf

Refrigerated biscuits are a nice accompaniment for an outdoor meal. Cinnamon rolls, buttermilk biscuits, and/or crescent rolls all require approximately the same amount of time on the grill. You can cook several at one time, if you wish.

- 1 package (any size) buttermilk biscuits, cinnamon rolls, or crescent rolls

Follow the package directions with regard to arranging the rolls on an aluminum foil pan. Set on the warming shelf on low, indirect heat, for 23 minutes, with the lid closed, and bake in the grill for 10 minutes. Spread with Honey Butter, if desired.

Honey Butter

- ½ cup (1 stick) butter or margarine at room temperature
- Honey to taste

Whip the butter with the honey, adding sufficient honey to sweeten to your taste.

CRISPY CORN PONE

Yield: 12–15 medium-sized muffins

Heat Control: low (2 burners), lid closed, warming shelf

Serve this with Honey Butter (below) for a spectacular taste treat.

- 1 egg
- ¾ cup milk
- 2 tablespoons vegetable oil
- 3 tablespoons sugar
- 1¼ cups biscuit mix
- ¾ cup cornmeal
- Honey Butter (below) (optional)

Combine egg, milk, and oil in a bowl, food processor, or blender and mix well. Add sugar, biscuit mix, and cornmeal. Stir until just blended. Do not overmix. Pour into well-greased muffin tins, ⅔ full. Place on the warming shelf with the heat set on low and the lid closed,

CINNAMON FRENCH TOAST

Yield: 6 servings

Heat Control: low, lid closed, direct heat

Ideal for breakfast or brunch on patio.

- 4 eggs
- ¼ teaspoon vanilla
- ¼ teaspoon cinnamon
- ¼ cup milk
- 6 thick slices French or sourdough bread
- 3 tablespoons melted butter or oil
- Powdered sugar (optional)

Beat together eggs, vanilla, cinnamon, and milk. Preheat a cast-iron skillet on the grill on high and reduce the heat to low. Dip the bread into the egg mixture, repeating if necessary, to use it all. Brush the skillet with butter and place the bread in it in a single layer. Close the grill lid and cook 3½ minutes per side. Transfer bread to a heated platter and sprinkle with powdered sugar, if desired. Serve with fresh strawberries, fruit, or maple syrup.

The selection of complementary vegetables and fruits is as important to a barbecue menu as the meat.

No barbecue experience is complete without traditional hot dogs and hamburgers. Char-grilling ensures juicy and flavorful results every time at home or on a picnic.

Variation: You may also use an aluminum foil pan, but do not preheat it. Cook for 2½ minutes on each side, with the grill lid closed.

APPLE PIE BROWNIES

Yield: 8 servings

Heat Control: low (1 burner), lid closed, indirect heat

These brownies are baked in an aluminum foil pie plate and cut into wedges.

- ¼ cup margarine, softened
- 1 cup sugar
- 1 egg
- 1 cup flour
- 1 teaspoon cinnamon
- ½ teaspoon nutmeg
- ½ teaspoon salt
- 1 teaspoon baking soda
- 2 tablespoons hot water
- 2 cups sliced apples
- ½ cup chopped walnuts or pecans

Cream together the margarine and sugar; add egg and mix well. Stir in flour, cinnamon, nutmeg, salt, and baking soda dissolved in water. Fold in the apples and nuts. Pour into a greased 9-inch aluminum foil pie plate. Bake on low (1 burner) over indirect heat, with the lid closed, for 45 minutes.

KENTUCKY DERBY PIE

Yield: 6–8 servings

Heat Control: low (1 burner), lid closed, indirect heat

This recipe shows the versatility of a gas grill.

- 1 cup sugar
- ½ cup flour
- 2 eggs, lightly beaten
- ½ cup melted butter, cooled
- 1 cup chopped pecans or English walnuts
- 1 cup semisweet chocolate chips
- 1 teaspoon vanilla
- 1 unbaked 9-inch deep dish pie shell

Mix together the sugar and flour; stir in the eggs and beat. Add butter, nuts, chocolate chips, and vanilla; blend well. Pour into the pie shell. Cook on low (1 burner), over indirect heat, with the lid closed, for 1 hour, or until a toothpick inserted in the center comes out clean.

Wok Cooking

9

ADD A NEW DIMENSION TO YOUR GRILL

Wok cooking is not only fun but convenient and very versatile, too. Although traditionally only Oriental dishes have been made in the wok, you will be surprised to learn that many Western-style dishes lend themselves well to preparation in your wok. You can use it for making all sorts of things, from New England Clam Chowder, to Texas or Mexican tacos, scrambled eggs, Italian Noodles Alfredo, and even toss a wilted spinach salad.

CHOOSING AND CARING FOR YOUR WOK

The traditional bowl-shaped wok is made of heavy-gauge rolled carbon steel, a metal that conducts heat well. Proper seasoning of the steel will keep it from rusting and will also keep foods from sticking to it. A new wok should be washed well in sudsy water, dried with a paper towel, and heated over your range, on your grill, or in a 400° F. oven for 20 minutes. With a paper towel, rub about 2 tablespoons of salad oil on the inside of your wok and continue heating for an additional 10 minutes. A flat-bottomed wok is best for grill cooking. Clean your wok with sudsy water after each use, scouring if necessary. Rub with oil before storing to prevent rusting.

HOW TO USE A WOK ON A GAS GRILL

Remove the grids from your grill and preheat the grill on high for about 5 minutes. For stir-frying, where intense heat is needed, move your briquets to the sides so that your wok will sit firmly on the grate, directly over the gas flames. Heat the skillet for 5 minutes, then add oil and continue heating with the grill lid closed, until oil ripples when the wok is tilted, approximately 5 minutes.

For food that needs to be cooked over a gentler heat, set your wok down directly on the briquets and preheat your pan with a tablespoon of oil for 5 minutes. During this time you can lower the grill lid on your wok. This helps heat the wok more quickly.

WOK COOKING TECHNIQUES

Stir-Frying

This is the traditional Oriental cooking method in which food is cut into small uniform slices, sometimes marinated, and then cooked quickly over high heat in a small amount of oil. With this quick method of cooking, vegetables remain bright and textures crisp, with nutrients intact. Meat, poultry, and fish are very tender, with juices retained. Because cooking times are very brief, it is necessary for the chef to remain at the grill, stirring and watching the food all the while.

All the ingredients should be prepared in advance and arranged in an attractive manner in separate bowls or platters, with the sauces and marinades accompanying them. Be sure to preheat your wok before adding oil. The oil should almost reach the smoking point before adding other ingredients. To test it, tilt the wok and check to see if the oil ripples. When it starts to ripple it is hot enough to start cooking.

All meats should be cut across the grain to make them more tender. (Freezing meats a half-hour before slicing helps in cutting thin and uniform slices.) Vegetables should be cut in a uniform pattern and size for even cooking. Vegetables such as broccoli and cauliflower should be steamed for a few minutes before stir-frying. This can be done early in the day. A very sharp knife or cleaver should be used for all cutting.

If you are stir-frying a large quantity, it is best either to prepare some of your food in advance and just reheat at serving time or to cook it in several smaller batches. Cooking very large quantities of meat at one time does not lend itself well to stir-frying.

Steaming

If you have room on your grill, you may wish to use half of it for steaming vegetables such as broccoli, asparagus, cauliflower, etc., in your wok. Steaming enhances the natural colors of your vegetables and retains all its nutrients. The important thing is to have all the vegetables in uniform size. You can do this in several ways. There are woven Oriental steamer baskets that fit into most woks and lend themselves to this type of food preparation. Stainless steel vegetable steamers and even metal colanders can also be used. Put your wok lid on top and steam.

(Above) An Oriental wok may be used on your gas-fired barbecue. Place the pan directly on the briquets. Add oil and preheat the pan on high before adding food. Almost all Oriental stir-fried recipes may be used.

SHRIMP IN THE WOK

Yield: 4 servings

Heat Control: *high and then medium, lid closed, wok on briquets*

Crunchy pea pods are a nice contrast to the shrimp in this Oriental-style entrée.

- 1 pound fresh jumbo shrimp
- 2 tablespoons cooking oil
- 1 5-ounce can sliced bamboo shoots, drained
- 4 scallions, sliced
- ⅓ pound pea pods
- ¾ cup chicken broth
- ¼ cup dry sherry
- 2 teaspoons soy sauce
- 1 teaspoon sugar
- 1 tablespoon wine vinegar
- 1 tablespoon cornstarch
- 1 teaspoon toasted sesame oil (see note below)

Shell and devein the shrimp. Butterfly the shrimp (cut lengthwise without cutting all the way through). Press flat with a knife or cleaver. Place the wok directly on the briquets, with the heat on high and the lid closed. Pour in the oil, close the lid, and heat until the oil is almost smoking. Add the bamboo shoots, scallions, and pea pods. Cook gently about 2 minutes, stirring often. Add shrimp, broth, sherry, soy sauce, and sugar, mixing well. Reduce the heat to medium and cook 5 minutes. Combine the vinegar and cornstarch and add to the shrimp, stirring constantly for about 1 minute or until the sauce thickens and clears. Add the sesame oil, stir, and serve immediately.

Note: Sesame oil is available in specialty and Oriental shops.

CHICKEN WITH DRY RED PEPPER

Yield: 3–4 servings

Heat Control: *high, lid open, wok on briquets*

A spicy chicken dish from northern China. If you are slightly timid, use fewer red peppers. Have all ingredients ready before you start stir-frying.

- 1 fryer chicken (about 2½–3 pounds) or 1 pound chicken breasts

Marinating Sauce
- 1 tablespoon soy sauce
- 1 tablespoon vegetable, corn, or peanut oil
- 1 tablespoon wine
- ⅛–¼ teaspoon crushed dried red pepper or 8 pieces dry red pepper (or fewer)
- ½ cup peanuts
- 1 tablespoon oil (or more)
- 1 teaspoon fresh grated or chopped ginger root
- 2 green onions or scallions
- 1 clove garlic, minced
- 1 cup pea pods, green pepper, broccoli, celery, or carrots

Seasoning Sauce
- 3 tablespoons soy sauce
- 1 tablespoon wine
- 1½ tablespoons cider vinegar
- 1 tablespoon cornstarch
- 1 tablespoon sugar
- ½ teaspoon salt (optional)
- 1 teaspoon sesame oil (or more)

Skin and bone the chicken and cut into 1-inch cubes. Combine soy sauce, 1 tablespoon oil, and wine. Pour over chicken, stir, and marinate for a half-hour.

If using whole dried peppers, wipe clean and remove the stems and seeds and cut into 1-inch-long pieces. Fry the peanuts in 1 tablespoon of oil in the wok, until golden, and remove them from the pan. Add more oil, if needed, and fry the chicken for a half-minute. Remove the chicken. Add more oil if needed.

Fry the red pepper until it turns black. Add the ginger, scallions, and garlic. Continue cooking for a few seconds, then add the vegetables and continue cooking until the vegetables are crunchy-tender. Add the cooked chicken and stir until reheated. Combine all the ingredients for Seasoning Sauce and pour over the vegetable and chicken mixture. Continue cooking until the mixture thickens and is heated through. Add peanuts, stir well, and serve immediately with rice.

MINCED PIGEON (CHICKEN BREASTS)

Yield: 4 servings or 12 appetizers
Heat Control: high, lid open, wok on briquets

Although pigeons are frequently served in China, in this country chicken is used. This dish is very tasty and tender, and it can be used as an appetizer or as one of several dishes in a Chinese meal.

1   chicken breast (2 halves)
6   ounces pork
4   dried mushrooms
1   fairly large onion, chopped
5   large fresh mushrooms
½   can (6 ounces) water chestnuts
½   can (6 ounces) bamboo shoots
Oil as needed
3   ounces rice noodles
15 large iceberg lettuce leaves

Meat Marinade
½   tablespoon soy sauce
1   egg yolk, with a little white
2   tablespoons cornstarch
½   teaspoon sugar

Seasoning Sauce
1   tablespoon soy sauce
1   tablespoon soup stock
1   tablespoon cornstarch
1   teaspoon sesame oil
¼   teaspoon pepper

Remove all bones from the chicken breast and cut the meat into small cubes. Do the same with the pork. Combine all the marinade ingredients in a bowl, pour over the chicken and pork, and marinate for about 10 minutes. Soak the dried mushrooms in warm water for about 10 minutes, discard the stems. Chop into small pieces. Chop the onion, fresh mushrooms, water chestnuts, and bamboo shoots. Heat the oil in the wok, set on the briquets for stir-frying, until very hot. Deep-fry the rice noodles until puffed and golden, only about 3 seconds on each side. Arrange on the bottom of a platter. Use additional oil and stir-fry the chicken and pork mixture until well done, about 3 minutes. Transfer to a bowl. Add additional oil, if needed, and stir-fry the onions until tender, then add mushrooms and stir-fry for another minute. Add the water chestnuts and bamboo shoots and stir-fry for 1 minute over high heat. Then add the meat mixture and the seasoning sauce. Stir until everything is heated through and the sauce has thickened. Pour over fried noodles and serve with lettuce leaves. To serve, tear large lettuce leaves in half and add approximately 1 tablespoon of rice-meat mixture. Wrap the lettuce leaf around this mixture when serving as an appetizer or a finger food. When serving as a main course, whole lettuce leaves arranged on a serving platter act as cups for individual portions.

Wok cooking is best done on warm and nonwindy days. The grill lid is open during a good portion of the cooking time. High winds tend to cool down the gas flames, making the intense heat necessary for stir-frying difficult to attain, if not impossible. Because of the large open surface of the wok, very cold weather tends to cool off surface ingredients too rapidly for proper quick cooking.

CHICKEN CHOW MEIN

Yield: 4 servings
Heat Control: high, lid open, wok on briquets

This is bound to become a family favorite. Serve with fried Rice Noodles (see recipe) or chow mein noodles.

- 2 tablespoons cooking oil
- 1 pound boneless chicken breasts or meat, slivered
- 2 onions, sliced
- 1 pound fresh Chinese vegetables (see note below) or bean sprouts
- 1 cup sliced celery
- 1 7-ounce can sliced water chestnuts
- 1 2-ounce jar pimientos, sliced
- 1 7/8-ounce package chicken gravy mix prepared according to directions on package
- 2 tablespoons soy sauce
- 1 teaspoon sugar

Remove the grill from the unit and place the wok directly on the briquets. Keep the heat set at high. Heat the oil in the wok and add the chicken meat, tossing quickly and cooking only until the meat has turned white. Remove the meat and reserve. Add a little additional oil, if necessary, and stir in the onions, Chinese vegetables, and celery. Stir until the vegetables are hot and steaming, about 10 minutes. Add the remaining ingredients and the chicken. Continue stirring until the mixture is hot again. Serve over chow mein noodles or hot rice as soon as the sauce comes to a boil.

(If the sauce is too thin, mix 1 tablespoon cornstarch with 2 tablespoons water and add a little at a time, until the sauce has thickened.)

Note: Chinese vegetables could include bok choy, snow peas, broccoli, etc., cut into uniform pieces if necessary.

MONGOLIAN BEEF

Yield: 4-6 servings
Heat Control: high, lid open, wok on briquets

This specialty of many Oriental restaurants is easily duplicated at home.

- 1-1½ pounds flank steak
- 1-2 tablespoons peanut oil

Meat Marinade
- ¼ cup white wine
- 1 tablespoon sesame oil
- 2 tablespoons soy sauce

Sauce
- 1 tablespoon cornstarch
- ¼ cup water
- 3 tablespoons Hoisin sauce
- 1 tablespoon Hot-Bean Sauce (see note)
- 1 teaspoon sesame oil
- 3 green onions

Freeze the flank steak for a half-hour until partially frozen; slice in very thin uniform slices with a sharp knife. Combine the wine, sesame oil, and soy sauce, and cover the flank steak in the marinade for at least 30 minutes. Combine all the ingredients for the sauce, including the onions, making sure the cornstarch is well dissolved. Set aside. Just before serving time, add 1 to 2 tablespoons of peanut oil to the wok, which has been placed in the briquets in the stir-frying position, as described in the beginning of this chapter. Heat it until very hot. Add the marinated meat and any leftover marinade and stir-fry until the red color leaves the steak. Add the sauce ingredients and continue cooking until thickened. Serve immediately over cooked rice or prepared rice noodles.

Note: Available in Oriental food stores.

BARBECUE SCRAMBLE

Yield: 4 servings

Heat Control: medium and then low, lid closed, wok on briquets

No need to cook eggs in the kitchen when everyone is out on the deck or patio.

- 6 eggs, beaten
- 1 cup diced cooked ham
- ¼ cup minced green onion
- ¼ cup sliced stuffed green olives (optional)
- ¼ cup diced green pepper
- ¼ teaspoon salt
- 2 tablespoons melted butter or oil
- 1 cup Charmglow Barbecue Sauce (see recipe) or prepared barbecue sauce (optional)

Combine eggs, ham, onion, olives, green pepper, and salt and set aside. Remove the grids from the grill. Preheat the grill on high for 5 minutes and reduce the heat to medium. Place a wok directly on the briquets and heat the butter or oil in it. Pour the egg mixture into wok and cook on low, with the lid closed, for about 7 minutes, until the egg mixture begins to set. Turn and finish by cooking for another minute. Transfer the egg mixture to heated plates and spoon the preheated sauce over the egg mixture, as desired.

RICE NOODLES IN WOK

Yield: 4–6 servings

Heat Control: high, lid open, wok on briquets

It's fascinating to watch the small noodles sizzle and pop up when cooked in hot oil.

- 2 cups peanut or vegetable oil
- ½ package (4 ounces) rice sticks

Rice noodles can be used in place of rice for stir-fried and other Oriental entrées.

Prepare wok as described in the introduction to this chapter. Heat the oil. Many Orientals can determine the proper oil temperature by putting a chopstick into the wok. When sufficient bubbles appear at the end of chopsticks, they know the oil is the proper temperature. This takes a bit of experience, however, and it is easier just to put a small crumb of rice sticks or rice noodles in your oil. If the oil is the proper temperature, it will puff up instantly when making contact with the oil. However, if the rice sticks just lie there and sizzle, continue heating the oil for several more minutes. When the oil is the proper temperature, throw a handful of rice sticks into the oil, let them puff up, and turn them, making sure that all the sticks have been immersed in the oil. Transfer to a paper towel–lined pan or platter. Continue this until sufficient rice sticks have been prepared for your meal. No need to worry about keeping these warm, as that is impossible. It takes approximately 12 minutes to heat oil in the wok to the proper temperature.

NOODLES ALFREDO

Yield: 4–6 servings

Heat Control: low, lid open, wok on grill

These noodles take a little bit more time to prepare than plain buttered noodles, but the difference in flavor makes them worth the effort.

- 1 8-ounce package medium-width egg noodles
- 4–5 cups chicken broth or 5 cups water mixed with 5 bouillon cubes
- ¼ cup butter
- Salt and pepper to taste
- ⅔ cup half-and-half
- ¾ cup freshly grated Parmesan cheese
- ½ cup snipped parsley

Cook the noodles in boiling broth or bouillon. When the noodles are al dente, drain. (Reserve the broth or bouillon for soups, gravies, etc.) Melt the butter in the wok on the grill over low heat. Add the noodles and toss gently to coat them. Add the half-and-half and continue cooking over low heat, tossing until it is completely absorbed. Add salt and pepper to taste. Remove the wok from grill, sprinkle the noodles with Parmesan cheese and parsley, and continue tossing until all the noodles are coated. Serve immediately.

FRESH ASPARAGUS IN WOK

Yield: 4–6 servings

Heat Control: high, lid open, wok on briquets

Stir-fried asparagus goes nicely with virtually every cuisine.

- 1 pound fresh asparagus
- 1 tablespoon salad oil
- ½ teaspoon grated fresh ginger
- 1 small clove garlic, minced
- 1 teaspoon soy sauce
- ½ teaspoon sesame oil (optional)

Wash the asparagus and break off the tough ends. Line up the asparagus in 1 bunch and with a cleaver cut diagonally into 1-inch pieces. Heat the wok and oil according to the instructions for stir-frying in the introduction to this chapter. When the oil is properly hot, add the ginger and garlic and cook for 30 seconds. Add the asparagus and continue cooking for 2–3 minutes, depending on the thickness of the asparagus. Add the soy sauce, stirring it into the asparagus, mix well, and add the sesame oil. Stir once more and serve immediately.

STIR-FRIED BEAN SPROUTS

Yield: 4 servings

Heat Control: high, lid open, wok on briquets

This is a wonderful vegetable recipe to accompany a grilled meat entrée.

- 1 tablespoon oil
- 1 pound bean sprouts
- 1 tablespoon soy sauce
- 1 teaspoon sugar
- Dash salt (optional)
- 1 teaspoon cornstarch
- 1 tablespoon water
- 1 teaspoon sesame oil

Add oil to a heated wok sitting on the briquets and cook on high until the oil is almost smoking. Add the bean sprouts and stir-fry briskly. Add the soy sauce, sugar, and a dash of salt, if desired; continue cooking over high heat for an additional minute. Combine cornstarch and water and pour over the sprouts. Cook until the liquid thickens, add the sesame oil, stir to mix, and then transfer to a serving platter and serve immediately.

WILTED SPINACH SALAD

Yield: 6 servings

Heat Control: high, lid open, wok on briquets

This German classic is cooked in the wok.

1 pound fresh spinach
8 slices bacon
¼ cup cider vinegar
3 teaspoons sugar
½ teaspoon salt
Dash freshly ground pepper
2 tablespoons bacon fat
4 scallions, snipped

Wash and dry the spinach; remove the coarse stems. Remove the grids from your grill and place a wok directly on the briquets. Sauté the bacon slices in the wok on high until crisp. Drain the bacon on a paper towel, reserving the fat. Combine the vinegar, sugar, salt, pepper, and bacon fat and bring to a boil in the wok. Cool. In a bowl, combine the scallions and crumbled bacon with the spinach. Toss the spinach mixture into the wok with the warm dressing. Toss and serve immediately while the dressing is warm (it need not be hot).

CHERRIES JUBILEE

Yield: 8 servings

Heat Control: low, lid open, wok on grill

Igniting these at night is truly spectacular. Your guests will be duly impressed.

2 10-ounce packages frozen dark sweet cherries
1 tablespoon sugar
2 teaspoons cornstarch
¼ cup kirsch or brandy

Thaw and drain the cherries, reserving the juice. In a wok, mix the sugar with the cornstarch. Add the cherry juice and place on the grill, with the heat on low, stirring until the liquid becomes thick and clear. Put the cherries into the wok and continue cooking until they are warmed. Pour the liqueur into a gravy ladle that is resting in the center of the wok, and heat for a minute or two. Let the kirsch or brandy run over the top of the gravy ladle into the cherry mixture. (This will keep the liqueur from mixing; it will lie on top of the cherry mixture.) Then ignite it; let the flame burn out or blow it out so that some of the alcohol remains. Spoon over vanilla ice cream and serve.

To flame outdoors can be a little bit difficult in gusty weather. It is best to add some pure-proof alcohol to your brandy for flaming purposes. Because of wind and other conditions, this is probably the only way to flame outside with certainty.

To flame outdoors can be a little difficult in gusty weather. It is best to add some pure-proof alcohol to your brandy for flaming purposes. Because of wind and other conditions, this is probably the only way to flame outside with certainty.

Smoker Cooking

10

SMOKE COOKING WITH A GAS GRILL

Because of the intense heat in a gas grill, wood chips tend to catch on fire and burn up without smoking. To avoid this, wrap the wet wood chips in heavy-duty foil in a cylinderlike shape, leaving the ends open. Place these foil packets directly on the briquets toward the front or the coolest part of your grill. The foil wrap around the wood keeps it from bursting into flame and allows it to smoke the way you want it to. Should the wood chips burst into flame, you can extinguish them with a water mister or baster. Be careful to use only a very small amount of water, just enough to put out the fire. These little packets of wood will eventually turn to ashes, but by that time sufficient smoke usually has been added to your food so that they need not be replaced. You can increase or decrease the intensity of the smoke flavor of your foods by taking one of the following steps.

- Place several packets of wood chips on your grill.
- Increase or decrease the amount of wood chips in each packet.
- Put a series of these packets on your grill, one after another. Replace with a fresh packet after all the wood chips have turned to ash and no longer emit smoke. Remove burned-up packets with tongs and place on nonflammable surface to cool.

The reason is unclear, but the smoked flavor of meats intensifies as it cools. When serving smoked meat the first day it will have a mild smoky flavor. Chill in refrigerator overnight and serve warm or cold the second day, and you will notice a more pronounced smoked flavor.

When smoking foods that have a shorter cooking time, such as Smoked Cheese, Beef Jerky, and Smoked Shrimp (see recipes), start the smoker unit about 10 minutes in advance so that the unit is fully smoking when the meat is added.

SMOKE COOKING WITH A WATER SMOKER

Smoke cooking is quite different from barbecuing on the conventional grill over direct heat, such as on a gas or charcoal grill. The water smoker is a hybrid of the American barbecue grill and the Chinese smoker. It has some of the features of a crockpot, an oven, a smokehouse, and a regular grill. Cooking is faster than in the old smokehouses but much slower than on a conventional grill.

These versatile units can be used in three different ways. You can grill directly above the heat source in much the same way as you would on a regular grill. You can use one as a water smoker, for which these units are most famous, or you can use it as a dry smoker, such as when making beef jerky. Cooking times will vary, depending not only on the outside temperature, but also on the wind velocity, as well as the elevation at which you are cooking. The fastest cooking is done at sea level in warm temperatures with no wind.

Hickory sticks, mesquite, or fruit woods are added to flavor the meat. Generally speaking, you are steaming your meat with the water cooker, which adds constant moisture to the heat. This is one reason the water smoker cooks lean meat so perfectly. A moist heat not only keeps the meat moist, but also tenderizes it.

Burning is not a problem with this type of cooking. Make sure that you always have water in your water pan, unless you are grilling directly over heat or dry-smoking meat such as beef jerky. The slow cooking will render most of the fat in your meat. This type of smoking flavors the meat rather than preserves it. Meat cooked in this manner should be served immediately and/or refrigerated promptly. Do not let cooked meat sit out.

The Water Pan

When using the water pan, always fill it with hot water. Marinades and other flavorings are often suggested as additions to the water, but our testing proves that this does very little for the flavor of the meat. It is best to add these flavorings, marinades, and/or basting sauces directly to the meat, rather than to the water pan. The water pan tempers the heat from your smoke cooker, creating a low moist and even heat that cooks the food gently and slowly. Drippings will collect in the pan. They can be concentrated, if necessary, by cooking them over moderate heat until the volume is reduced to the desired concentration. Use these drippings as a base for soups, sauces, and gravies. If there is a lot of fat accumulation, skim before using.

Timing Is Important

Smoke cooking is easy and does not require a lot of attention. The biggest adjustment is to realize that with this method, it is going to take a much longer time to cook an item than it would on a conventional grill. To shorten the cooking time, always have meat at room temperature before smoke cooking. Add hot or boiling water to the water pan. Do this after the water pan is in place. Since overcooking is not likely, allow plenty of cooking time. It is always best to allow more time than needed rather than too little. Wind and weather conditions can change, increasing or decreasing your smoke cooking time.

To shorten the cooking time of a large piece of meat such as turkey, you can start it in your microwave oven and finish it in the water smoker. Your bird will still have that delectable smoky flavor. Two 12-pound turkeys will cook in almost half the time that it would take a 24-pound turkey to cook. For large quantities you may wish to use several smaller pieces of meat instead of one very large one.

Opening and Closing Your Water Smoker

Particularly in the beginning, you will have a strong urge to open the water smoker frequently to check on your meat. However strong this urge is, try to resist it. Just as in crockpot cooking, lifting the lid for a quick peek is verboten! Every time you lift the lid a large amount of heat escapes, which in turn will take your water smoker approximately 10 minutes to replace. (This is in warm weather with no wind. In colder temperatures or on a windy day 15–20 minutes would be needed.) Always be sure to use heat-resistant mitts when removing water pan during smoking process.

For larger pieces of meat, refill the water pan after 3 hours. Refill the water pan with hot water, if you

The temperature at the top level of your gas smoker is about 235°F., whereas the temperature on the bottom level, closer to the source of the heat, is about 320°F. Electric smokers run hotter, at about 363°F.

are in a hurry, or else add 30 minutes to your cooking time. Also use this opportunity to check the meat thermometer and/or to baste meats. Using a meat thermometer is the best way to determine when the meat is finished.

Flavoring the Meat

Marvelous smoke flavors can be obtained from wood chips made of fruit and nut woods, such as hickory, pecan, walnut, apple, cherry, and mesquite. Never use resinous wood such as pine, as it can impart a bitter and turpentinelike flavor to your food. When using wood, soak chips in water for at least one hour or overnight.

As mentioned earlier, it is often noted in water smoker directions that flavoring can be added to the water pan. However, we have found after much experimentation that any flavor you wish to add to the meat is best added directly to the meat. Marinades, barbecue sauces, herbs, and seasonings are best brushed and/or basted directly onto the meat. Adding barbecue sauces, marinades, and other flavor enhancers to your water pan does impart a marvelous aroma to your outdoor cooking area, but adds little flavor to your meat. Meats can often be marinated overnight in your refrigerator. This can have a tenderizing effect on the meat as well as enhancing flavor.

Cleaning Your Water Smoker

Both the grill and the water pans are easy to clean with mild soap and water or in your dishwasher. Smoke accumulating on the inside of your water smoker is natural and does not need to be cleaned off or scoured. An occasional wipe with a sudsy cloth on the outside of your water smoker, followed by a rinse with clear water, will keep your water smoker looking bright and beautiful.

Smoker Cooking Chart*

Meat	Size or Weight	Heat Control	Time
BEEF			
Rump Roast	2½–4 lbs.	High/with water	6 hrs. or 2 hrs. 10 min. per lb.
Sirloin Tip Roast	4–5 lbs.	High/with water	5½ hrs. or 1 hr. 20 min. per lb.
Flank Steak	1½–2 lb. pieces	High/with water	1½ hrs. per lb.
Short Ribs	any amount	High/with water	5 hrs.
Meat Loaf	3-lb. loaves	High/with water	3 hrs.
Corned Beef	2½–3½ lbs.	High/with water	1 hr. 45 min. per lb.
PORK			
Pork Roast	3–6 lbs.	High/with water	1 hr. 20 min. per lb.
Stuffed Pork Chops	¾" thick	High/with water	2 hrs.
Smoked Barbecued Pork Roast	3–4 lbs.	High/with water	50 min. per lb.
Pork Roast (with bone in)	6 lbs.	High/with water	2½ hrs. per lb.

To use the versatile wok with your gas grill, remove the grids from the grill and place the wok directly over the gas flames.

Smoked whole turkey can be served hot or cold. Make several at once (one on each level) and freeze the extras for future meals.

Meat	Size or Weight	Heat Control	Time
Spareribs	any amount	High/with water	3 hrs.
Baby Back Ribs	any amount	High/with water	3 hrs.
Back Ribs	any amount	High/with water	3 hrs.
Sausage, Smoked (fresh)	any amount	High/with water	1 hr.
Ham, Fresh, bone in	any amount	High/with water	2½ hr. per lb.
Precooked	any amount	High/with water	24 min. per lb.
POULTRY			
Chicken—Whole	3–4 lbs.	High/with water	3–3½ hrs. or 45 min. per lb.
Turkey Legs	any amount	High/with water	5 hrs.
Breast	5½–6 lbs.	High/with water	9½ hrs. or 1 hr. 30 min. per lb.
Wings	4 wings—1 lb. each	High/with water	5 hrs.
Whole	10–12 lbs.	High/with water	10 hrs. or 1 hr. per lb.
Pheasant		High/with water	5 hrs.
Wild Duck	1 medium	High/with water	5 hrs.
Duckling	5 lbs.	High/with water	5½ hrs. or 1 hr. 10 min. per lb.
SEAFOOD			
King Crab Legs	3 lbs.	High/with water	1 hr.
Pan Fish	small	High/with water	30 min.
Salmon Steaks	1″ thick	High/with water	1 hr.
Shrimp	medium	Low/lid closed (on foil)	20–25 min.
Trout	whole (14–16 oz. ea.)	High/with water	1 hr.
VEGETABLES			
Corn in Husks		High/with water	1½–2 hrs.
Mushrooms	large	High/with water	45 min. to 1 hr.
Spanish Onions	2 large	High/with water	2–2½ hrs.
Potatoes, Red	small to medium	High/with water	1 hr.
Zucchini	small, tender, cut in half	High/with water	1½ hrs.
APPETIZERS			
Beef Jerky	2 lbs.	High/with water	1 hr.
Smoked Cheese	8 oz.	High/without water (on foil)	45 min. to 1 hr.
Smoked Almonds/Pecans	5½ oz. ea.	High/with water	2 hrs.

* All times are for gas smoker unit. Electric smoker units cook approximately 10%–15% faster than gas smokers, so a proportionately shorter cooking time is required.

All cooking times in recipes are for gas smoker units. Reduce cooking time 10-15% for electric smoker units.

BEEF

ROLLED SIRLOIN TIP (ITALIAN-STYLE)

Yield: 8 servings

Heat Control: high, water pan full

Surprisingly, this recipe tastes better the second day, and it makes marvelous sliced beef sandwiches.

- 1 4- to 5-pound rolled sirloin tip beef roast
- 2 cloves garlic
- ½ medium onion
- 1½ teaspoons oregano
- Salt, as desired

Make about 10 slits in the roast. Insert small pieces of fresh garlic, onion, and oregano. Lightly sprinkle oregano over the roast according to your own taste. Use a meat thermometer to determine the internal temperature of the meat. Place soaked wood chips in place. Fill the water pan with hot water. Put the grill in place and the roast in the center. It will take approximately 5½ hours for medium-rare.

PUNGENT SMOKY FLANK STEAK

Yield: 6–8 servings

Heat Control: high, water pan ¾ full

This marinated steak should be sliced on the diagonal to ensure tenderness.

- ¼ cup soy sauce
- 3 tablespoons honey
- 2 tablespoons vinegar
- ½ teaspoon garlic powder
- ½ teaspoon ground ginger
- ¾ cup salad oil
- 2 green onions, finely chopped
- 1 flank steak (about 2 pounds)

Combine all ingredients except the steak. Let sit for about 1 hour. Pour the mixture over the steak and marinate overnight. When ready to cook, place the steak on grill and smoke for 2 hours for medium-well. Baste with the marinade before serving and slice on the diagonal.

SMOKED MEAT LOAF

Yield: 6 individual loaves, about ½ pound each

Heat Control: high, water pan full

Making these into individual loaves speeds up cooking time and increases the smoke penetration. Make a double batch and freeze for future meals. This is great when warmed in a microwave.

- 1 slice white bread, crust removed
- ¼ cup milk
- 1 pound ground pork and 2 pounds ground beef or 1 pound ground beef, 1 pound ground pork, and 1 pound ground veal
- 2 eggs
- ¾ cup chopped onion
- 1 teaspoon beef bouillon
- ¼ cup chopped parsley
- ½ cup finely chopped celery
- ¼ teaspoon poultry seasoning
- ¼ teaspoon garlic powder
- ½ teaspoon salt

Tear or crumble the bread and add to the milk. Combine the remaining ingredients, then add the milk mixture and mix well. Shape into 6 individual loaves, approximately 9 ounces each. Fill water pan with hot water. Put loaves on aluminum trays and place in the smoker for approximately 3 hours. Baste once or twice with juices from pan.

BEEF JERKY

Yield: about 1½ pounds
Heat Control: high, water pan ¾ full

Beef jerky makes a nice snack or appetizer and is great for picnics, camping, and backpacking trips.

2 **pounds flank steak**
⅓ **cup soy sauce**
1 **clove garlic, minced (optional)**

Trim all visible fat from the steak (jerky keeps indefinitely if all fat is trimmed). Cut the flank steak lengthwise with the grain, into long thin strips, ¼ inch thick. Place the strips in a bowl, pour soy sauce over the meat, and toss several times. Marinate for 15 minutes. Place on racks in the smoker, leaving a small space in between slices. Smoke-cook 1 hour. Refrigerate.

SMOKED CORNED BEEF

Yield: 6-8 servings
Heat Control: high, water pan almost full

This makes especially good sandwiches.

1 **2½- to 3½-pound corned beef brisket for oven roasting**
¼ **cup water**
1 **large bay leaf, broken into pieces**
½ **teaspoon peppercorns**
1 **clove garlic, chopped**

Tear off an 18-inch piece of heavy-duty foil. Fold up the edges slightly, making a drip pan, or use a foil pan. Remove the corned beef brisket from its wrapping. Rinse thoroughly and place the brisket in the center of the foil. Add 2 or 3 chunks of soaked wood to bottom of smoker. Put the water pan in place and fill almost full with hot water. Put the cooking grill in place. Place the foil tray or pan with the brisket in the center of the cooking grill. Combine water and seasonings and pour over the brisket. Cover and start the unit. Smoke-cook about 5½ hours on high. After about 4 hours, you may need to check the water pan and add a quart or more of hot water.

(Above) One and a half hours before the corned beef has finished cooking, fill the water pan with fresh, hot seasoned water or broth and add cut-up cabbage or potatoes or both.

HERBED BEEF SHORT RIBS

Yield: 6 servings

Heat Control: high, water pan full

If you like your meat to fall off the bone, add an extra hour of cooking.

5–6 pounds beef short ribs, about 2½ inches thick
¼ cup vegetable oil
1 tablespoon Worcestershire sauce
⅓ cup red dry wine
⅓ cup vinegar
2 tablespoons mustard
1 teaspoon garlic powder
1 teaspoon dried dill
5–6 drops Tabasco sauce

Put the ribs in a baking dish, bowl, or heavy-duty plastic bag. In a small bowl or a measuring cup, combine all the remaining ingredients and blend. Pour the marinade over the ribs. Turn the ribs to coat them completely with the marinade. Cover with plastic wrap or close the bag securely. Refrigerate at least several hours, preferably overnight, turning occasionally.

Remove the meat from the refrigerator. Place 2 or 3 chunks of soaked wood in the smoker unit. Put the water pan in place and fill it with hot water. Put the cooking grill in place. Lift the ribs from the marinade and put them on the cooking grill. Pour the marinade over the meat and let drip into the water pan. Cover. Smoke-cook about 5 hours, or until the meat is tender. After about 4 hours you may need to check the water pan and add a quart of hot water.

PORK

SMOKED SAUSAGE WITHOUT CASINGS

Yield: 2½ pounds uncooked sausage

Heat Control: high, water pan ½ full

You'll find many different ways of using these sausages. One of our favorites is to slice it thin and serve it with fresh spaghetti, a basil sauce, and Parmesan cheese. This is also good in quiche, hot potato salad, etc.

Sausage
1½ cups parsley leaves
3 large cloves garlic, peeled
½ small onion
2 slices (2 ounces) good-quality white bread, broken into pieces
½ pound lean veal, cut into 1-inch cubes, semifrozen
1 pound lean pork loin, cut into 1-inch cubes, semifrozen
¾ pound pork fat, cut into 1-inch cubes, semifrozen
2 tablespoons nonfat dry milk powder
1 tablespoon Seasoning Salt (below)
¾ teaspoon coarsely ground pepper

Meat Grinder Method: Put the meat through a food grinder along with the bread and seasonings. You may wish to put the meat through the coarse grinder first and then the fine grinder. (This helps mix the ingredients evenly.) If further blending is necessary, use your hands.

Food Processor Method: Using the metal blade in the food processor, add the parsley to the work bowl and process until finely minced. With the machine running, drop the garlic and onion through the feed tube and process until finely minced. Add the bread and process 10 seconds until the bread is finely chopped. Remove the herb-crumb mixture from the work bowl and set aside. Toss the pork loin, veal, and fat together and put them into the work bowl with the milk powder, Seasoning Salt, and pepper. Pulse 8 times and then process 25 seconds, until the meat is finely chopped. Distribute the herb-crumb mixture evenly over the meat and process for 10 seconds until all the ingredients are well mixed. Remove the mixture from the work bowl.

Divide the meat mix into 10 equal parts. Shape into a smooth cylinder about 2 inches thick. Place sausage on grill with half-filled water pan in place. Smoke-cook for one hour. The rendered pork fat will baste these sausages as they cook.

Seasoning Salt

Yield: about ⅓ cup

- ¼ cup salt
- 1 teaspoon dried tarragon
- 1 teaspoon dried basil
- 2 teaspoons Hungarian paprika
- 1 teaspoon ground coriander
- ½ teaspoon cinnamon
- ½ teaspoon mace
- ½ teaspoon freshly ground nutmeg
- ¼ teaspoon dried marjoram

In a small bowl, stir together the salt, tarragon, basil, paprika, coriander, cinnamon, mace, nutmeg, and marjoram. Makes about ⅓ cup.

STUFFED PORK CHOPS

Yield: 3 servings (1 pork chop per serving)
Heat Control: high, water pan ¾ full

Hearty appetites will enjoy these moist and fruity pork chops.

- 3 ¾-inch pork chops with pocket
- 1 cup apple juice
- 4 slices bread, crumbled
- 1 tablespoon chopped onion
- ½ cup chopped apples
- ¼ cup white raisins
- ⅛ teaspoon pepper
- ⅛ teaspoon sage
- 1 egg

Marinate the pork chops in the apple juice for a half-hour. Mix the remaining ingredients and stuff into the pocket of pork chops. Fill water pan ¾ full with hot water. Smoke-cook on the grill for 2 hours.

SMOKED BARBECUED PORK ROAST

Yield: about 7–9 servings
Heat Control: high, water pan full

Leftovers make fantastic sandwiches. You may wish to make several at one time and freeze them for future meals.

- 1 3- to 4-pound lean rolled pork roast
- Barbecue sauce
- Chopped parsley

Brush the roast generously with barbecue sauce and sprinkle with chopped parsley. Fill water pan. Smoke-cook 3–4 hours. Use a meat thermometer to check for doneness.

PORK ROAST

Yield: about 6 servings

Heat Control: high, water pan almost full

Although not as easy to carve as a rolled pork roast, you'll find the bone adds considerable flavor to the meat.

1	3-pound pork loin roast, bone in
2	teaspoons dried dill
2	teaspoons caraway seed

Sprinkle the pork roast with the dill and caraway seed. Place on the grill on high, with a water pan almost full. Cook approximately 4 hours (1 hour and 20 minutes per pound).

BOHEMIAN PORK ROAST

Yield: 8 servings

Heat Control: high, water pan almost full

This roast is a complete meal—great for the busy person!

1	6-pound pork loin roast (with bone)
2	pounds sauerkraut
2	apples, cored and chopped
5	slices bacon, cut into 1-inch pieces
1	cup dry white wine or apple juice (or more)
1	tablespoon caraway seed
½	teaspoon celery salt
1	quart hot water (or more)

Insert a meat thermometer into the center of the largest muscle of the roast. Make sure the thermometer doesn't touch the bone. Add 2 or 3 chunks of soaked wood to the grill. Set the water pan in place and add enough hot water to fill almost full. Put the cooking grill in place. Place the meat in the center of the cooking grill. Cover. Smoke-cook about 7½ hours, or until the meat thermometer reaches 170° F. In the meantime, combine the sauerkraut, apples, bacon, and seasonings and set aside. After about 4 hours, remove the water pan and add the sauerkraut mixture with 1 quart of hot water. Return the water pan with the sauerkraut mixture to the smoker, replace the meat, and continue cooking. Check the sauerkraut after 2 hours to make sure it hasn't dried out. Add more wine or water, as needed.

BAVARIAN RIBS AND KRAUT

Yield: 6–8 servings

Heat Control: high, water pan full

Meat and vegetables are all cooked on your smoker unit in this recipe.

6	pounds spareribs
2	1-pound cans sauerkraut
½	cup chopped onion
1	cup white wine
2	tablespoons brown sugar
1	tablespoon caraway seed
8	or more small whole new potatoes (optional)
1	quart water

Remove the ribs from the refrigerator an hour or so before smoking, so they will be at room temperature. Place 2 or 3 chunks of soaked wood in the bottom of the smoker. Put the water pan in place and add just enough water to fill. Put the cooking grill in place. Arrange the ribs on the cooking grill or in a rib rack on the cooking grill. Cover and start smoker unit. Ribs will take about 3½–4 hours. Meanwhile, combine the sauerkraut, onion, and all the remaining ingredients and place in an oven-proof casserole dish. After about 2 hours, add more hot water to the water pan, if needed. Place the sauerkraut mixture and potatoes in an uncovered casserole on lower grill. Smoke-cook an additional 1½–2 hours. Check casserole dish after 1 hour, adding more water if necessary, to keep the kraut very moist. Serve the ribs with the kraut and potatoes.

LEMON-DILL BACK RIBS

Yield: 6 servings
Heat Control: high, water pan almost full

The slow smoke-cooking renders all the fat from the ribs.

4 pounds back ribs
3 lemons
1 teaspoon sugar
1 teaspoon oil
¼ teaspoon salt
½ teaspoon dried dillweed or caraway seed
¼ teaspoon basil
2 drops red pepper sauce

Arrange the ribs in a baking dish or in a heavy-duty plastic bag. Grate the peel from 1 of the lemons and reserve. Juice all 3 lemons. Combine the grated lemon peel, juice, and all the remaining ingredients in a small bowl and pour over the ribs. Cover with plastic wrap or close the bag securely and marinate for about 1 hour at room temperature.

Add 2 or 3 chunks of soaked wood to bottom of grill. Put the water pan in place and fill almost full of hot water. Set the cooking grill in place. Arrange the ribs on the grill. Pour the marinade over the ribs and let drip into the water pan. Cover. Start the smoker unit. Smoke-cook about 3 hours.

SPARERIBS

Yield: 2 entrée servings
Heat Control: high, without water

These ribs are cooked very slowly over direct heat in your smoker unit.

2 pounds spareribs (see note below)
⅓ cup barbecue sauce

Cook the spareribs directly on the grill over the heat source, on high, without water pan, for 1¼ hours. Spread with barbecue sauce, turning once. Serve with additional barbecue sauce.

Note: Back ribs take longer to cook via this method and tend to dry out; not recommended.

BABY BACK RIBS

Yield: 2–4 servings (½–¾ pound per serving)
Heat Control: high, water pan almost full

This basic rib recipe requires no preparation.

1–2 pounds baby back ribs
1 recipe Charmglow Bar-B-Q-Sauce (see recipe)

Fill water pan. Brush the ribs generously with Charmglow Bar-B-Q-Sauce and smoke-cook for approximately 3 hours. Brush with additional sauce after 2 hours and check the water pan.

EXTRA-SPECIAL BARBECUED SPARERIBS

Yield: 5–6 servings

Heat Control: high, water pan full

All the ingredients in this basting sauce can be combined in a blender.

1 cup chopped onion
1 cup ketchup
½ cup water
1 teaspoon salt
2 tablespoons Worcestershire sauce
⅓ cup vinegar
⅓ cup brown sugar
2 teaspoons dry mustard
1 teaspoon paprika
4–5 pounds pork spareribs

Combine all ingredients for sauce and simmer for 5 minutes. Cut the meat into serving pieces and place in a very large shallow baking dish or foil pan. Put soaked wood in place. Fill the water pan with hot water. Pour the sauce over the ribs. Smoke-cook 3 hours or until tender.

POULTRY

PHEASANT

Yield: 3–4 servings

Heat Control: high, water pan full

Fill your smoker with a number of pheasants at one time. These are good as an entrée but are especially good served cold and sliced with horseradish sauce.

2 pheasants, fully dressed
1 quart water
¼ cup salt
12 juniper berries
4 small onions, quartered
Several sprigs parsley
4 tablespoons butter or margarine

Rinse and drain birds with cold water, then let them stand, uncovered, at room temperature, while starting the smoker unit. Add 2 or 3 chunks of soaked wood to the smoker. Insert the water pan and fill it with hot water. Set the cooking grill in place.

Put juniper berries, onion, and parsley in the cavity of the bird. Brush generously with butter. Arrange the bird on the cooking grill. Cover. Smoke-cook about 5 hours, depending on the size of the bird, or until a leg twists easily in its socket. Baste the pheasant halfway through and add hot water to pan.

FRUIT-ROASTED PHEASANT

Yield: 2–4 servings

Heat Control: high, water pan full

The sauce keeps the pheasant moist while imparting a pleasant fruit flavor.

1 pheasant
Salt and pepper
½ cup white rice
½ cup brown rice
1 cup apricot juice

Place the pheasant on an aluminum foil pan. Rub the interior with salt and pepper; cover with uncooked rice. Pour the fruit juice over all. Fill water pan with hot water. Smoke-cook for 4 hours, or until the pheasant can easily be pierced with a fork.

SMOKED WHOLE TURKEY

Yield: 13–16 servings
Heat Control: high, water pan full

When served cold the next day, the smoked flavor of this meat is much stronger. Try prepared horseradish sauce with it as a condiment.

1   10- to 12-pound turkey
Butter
Salt and pepper
2   ribs celery, chopped
1   medium onion, chopped
1   large bay leaf, crumbled

Rub the inside of the turkey generously with butter, then rub salt and pepper inside the turkey. Stuff with celery, onion, and bay leaf. Place on the lower grill with the water pan filled and in place. Cook on high for about 10 hours, or until the meat thermometer reaches 180° F. Check the water pan every 4 hours and refill with hot water.

SMOKED TURKEY BREAST

Yield: about 9 servings
Heat Control: high, water pan full

Because this size breast comes from a turkey weighing approximately 12 pounds, the breast alone will take just as long to smoke-cook as a whole turkey. Smoke several at one time and freeze extras. White meat will be moist and juicy.

1   3-pound turkey breast
Butter

Place the turkey breast skin side down on the upper grill. Cook on high, with a full water pan. Smoke-cook about 10 hours, basting with butter after 3 hours.

ULTIMATE SMOKED TURKEY BREAST

Yield: 10–12 servings
Heat Control: high, water pan full

Delicious hot or cold—great in a Hawaiian turkey salad with pineapple.

1   turkey breast (bone in, not rolled), approximately 5½–6 pounds

Teriyaki Sauce
¼   cup soy sauce
½   cup sherry
¼   cup oil
1   tablespoon ginger
1   tablespoon dry mustard
1   teaspoon garlic powder

Combine the Teriyaki Sauce ingredients. Rinse the turkey breast and place in a covered bowl or plastic bag. Pour the sauce over it and marinate overnight, turning several times. Put 2 or 3 soaked wood chunks in place. Fill the water pan with hot water. Grease the grill to prevent sticking. Put the turkey breast in the center of the grill. Put the cover on the smoker unit and ignite. Baste the turkey breast with the remaining sauce every three hours and refill the water pan with hot water. Smoke-cook about 9½ hours. When the turkey is done, liberally brush again and allow to smoke for 15 minutes more. For a stronger smoked flavor, serve on the second day.

> Smoke flavor can be intensified over a long cooking time by adding soaked woods during cooking.

TURKEY WINGS WITH DRESSING

Yield: 6 servings

Heat Control: high, water pan full

There is a surprisingly generous amount of meat on a turkey wing—a terrific budget stretcher.

- 4 turkey wings, about 1 pound each
- 3 cups dressing

Dressing
- ½ pound ground chuck or pork sausage
- ½ cup chopped onion
- ½ cup chopped celery
- 12 slices dry bread
- 1 teaspoon salt
- 1 teaspoon poultry seasoning
- 2 eggs

For the dressing, sauté the meat, onion, and celery just until the meat starts to turn gray in color. Pour this mixture over the bread, which has been soaked in water and pressed out. Add the seasonings and egg and mix well. Assemble the turkey wings with the dressing.

Put two turkey wings, outer side down, and place half the dressing on each wing. Place remaining wings on top.

Smoke-cook the stuffed wings approximately 5 hours on the high setting, with the water pan filled. Slice the turkey wings with a carving knife parallel to the bone, through both wings and dressing.

ORIENTAL TURKEY LEGS

Yield: 6-8 servings

Heat Control: high, water pan full

A great way to use economical turkey legs.

- 4-6 turkey legs
- 1 envelope onion soup mix
- ½ cup oil
- 1 cup cider vinegar
- ½ cup soy sauce
- ½ teaspoon garlic powder
- 2 teaspoons fresh ginger root, grated
- 1 tablespoon sesame seeds

Place the turkey legs in a heavy-duty plastic bag. Combine all the remaining ingredients, except the sesame seeds, and pour them over the turkey. Close the bag securely and refrigerate overnight, turning the legs occasionally.

Remove the turkey legs from the refrigerator. Place 2 or 3 chunks of soaked wood in the bottom of the smoker unit. Put the water pan in place and fill almost full of hot water. Put the cooking grill in place. Arrange the turkey legs on the grill. Pour the excess marinade over and let it drip into the water pan. Sprinkle the legs with the sesame seeds. Cover and smoke-cook for about 5 hours. After about 4 hours you may need to check the water pan and add a quart or so of hot water.

SMOKED DUCK WITH ORANGE SAUCE

Yield: 3-4 servings

Heat Control: high, water pan full

Frozen orange juice concentrate simplifies this classic recipe.

- 1 5-pound duckling
- 1 cup frozen orange juice concentrate
- ½ cup soy sauce
- ¼ cup sherry
- 1 clove garlic, minced
- 1 teaspoon dry mustard
- ½ teaspoon cayenne sauce

Put the duckling into a glass bowl or heavy-duty plastic bag. Combine all the remaining ingredients in a small bowl and pour over the duckling, being sure the marinade goes all over the inside as well as the outside of the bird. Cover the bowl with plastic wrap or close the bag securely. Refrigerate overnight or at least for several hours, turning the duckling in the marinade several times. Remove the duckling from the refrigerator.

Place 2 or 3 chunks of soaked wood in the bottom of smoker. Put the water pan in place and fill almost full of hot water. Set the cooking grill in place. Lift the duckling from the bag to the center of the lower cooking grill. Prick the surface of the duckling in many places with a two-tined fork, so the fat can drain off. Pour the marinade over the duckling. Cover and start the smoker unit. Smoke-cook about 3½ hours or until a duck leg twists easily in its socket. After about 2 hours, baste the duckling and check the water pan; additional hot water may be needed.

Before serving, heat any remaining orange sauce in a small saucepan or in a microwave in an appropriate container. Pour over the carved duck or serve separately.

WILD DUCK WITH ORANGE SAUCE

Yield: 2 servings

Heat Control: high, water pan full

This is great served with wild or brown rice.

1   **medium or large wild duck**
Salt
1   **apple, cored and quartered**
1   **tablespoon butter**
¼   **cup honey**
¼   **cup orange juice**
1   **teaspoon orange peel**
¼   **teaspoon ginger**
¼   **teaspoon basil leaves**

To minimize the wild flavor of the duck, you may wish to soak the bird in salted water overnight. Wash the duck and dry with a paper towel. Salt the body cavity; stuff the duck with apple quarters. In a small saucepan, heat the remaining ingredients until the butter melts. Place the duck in a shallow pan or on a piece of heavy-duty foil large enough to fold completely around the duck. Pour ⅓ of the heated sauce into the cavity and ⅓ over the duck. Seal all the edges of the foil so the liquid does not drain out. Fill the water pan. Smoke-cook for 5 hours. Discard the apple and slice the meat. Serve with the remaining sauce.

SMOKED WHOLE CHICKEN

Yield: about 3 servings

Heat Control: high, water pan full

Moist and tender—no sauces needed. This is delicious cold, so make several at one time.

1   **3- to 4-pound chicken**
Salt (optional)
1   **rib celery, with tops**
2   **slices onion**
1   **small bay leaf**

Rinse the chicken and blot dry. Rub the cavity lightly with salt, if you wish. Place the celery, onion, and bay leaf in the cavity. Set the water pan in place and fill. Put the grill in place and set the prepared chicken on the grill. Smoke-cook for approximately 3-3½ hours.

SMOKED CHICKEN TERIYAKI

Yield: 4 servings

Heat Control: high, water pan almost full

Dress up plain chicken with this teriyaki sauce. It's very moist, with a very definite Oriental flavor.

- 1 3-pound chicken
- ⅓ cup soy sauce
- ¼ cup sherry
- ½ teaspoon garlic powder
- 1½ teaspoons ginger
- 1½ teaspoons dry mustard

Arrange the whole chicken or chicken pieces in a baking dish or heavy-duty plastic bag. Combine all the remaining ingredients in a small bowl until blended. Pour the marinade into and over the chicken. Turn the chicken so the marinade coats it completely. Cover with plastic wrap or close the bag securely. Refrigerate overnight, occasionally turning the chicken in the marinade. Remove the chicken from the refrigerator.

Place 2 or 3 chunks of wood that have been soaked in water in the bottom of the smoker. Put the water pan in place and fill almost full of hot water. Put the cooking grill in place. Lift the chicken from the marinade and place it on the cooking grill. If you want, insert a meat thermometer in the thickest part of the thigh, away from the bone. If you have cut-up chicken, try to leave some space between the pieces. Pour the marinade over the chicken and let it drip into the water pan. Cover and start the smoker. Smoke-cook a whole chicken for about 3½ hours, or until the meat thermometer reaches 180° F. Smoke-cook chicken pieces for 2½ hours. Check the water pan every 3 hours and add a quart or so of hot water, if necessary.

FISH AND SEAFOOD

PAN FISH

Yield: 4–6 servings

Heat Control: high, water pan ½ full

Because these fish are in the smoker unit for such a short time, it is best to start the unit 10 minutes before placing them on the grill. This will give the smoker ample time to start smoking before the fish are placed on the grill.

- 6 small whole pan fish, fresh or thawed and cleaned (perch, sunfish, bluegills)
- Freshly ground pepper or lemon pepper
- ¼ cup oil

Put wood chips in place. Set the water pan in place and fill with hot water, about ½ full. Sprinkle the cavities of the fish with pepper or lemon pepper. Brush the outsides of the fish with oil. Start the unit so that it will be smoking properly when the pan fish are added. With the cooking grill in place, arrange the fish on the lower grill. Cover. Smoke-cook about 30 minutes, or until the fish flakes when tested with a fork. Serve with tartar sauce.

WHITE FISH MOUSSE

Yield: 8–10 appetizer or first course servings

Heat Control: high, water pan ¾ full

Serve this as a first course or appetizer.

1½ pounds white fish fillet, skins removed
½ cup egg whites
1 cup cream
½ teaspoon white pepper
Dash seasonings
Watercress or parsley

Line a loaf pan with greased parchment paper. With the metal blade in a food processor, process the white fish fillet, from which the bone has been removed, until finely chopped. In a separate bowl, beat the egg whites until quite stiff. Add the cream to the fish mixture in the processor and continue to process until the mixture is very smooth. Add the seasonings. Fold into the egg white mixture and pour into a prepared pan. Put the loaf pan on the cooking grill. Cover grill and smoke-cook with water pan ¾ full, for about 2 hours. Remove from the grill and let sit about 10 minutes before unmolding. This can be served warm or cold and will freeze well.

SMOKED SALMON

Yield: ⅓ pound per person
Heat Control: high, water pan ½ full for steaks, almost full for whole fish

This very expensive delicacy can be made easily and economically at home.

Fresh salmon steaks (about 1 inch thick) or 1 whole salmon
Melted butter
Lemon juice
Dill, to taste, preferably fresh

Salmon Steaks: Combine equal parts of butter and lemon juice, and brush each steak on both sides with the mixture. Sprinkle with dill.

Whole Salmon: Brush the salmon cavity with the butter-lemon mixture and sprinkle with dill. Repeat on the outside of the salmon.

Place the briquets and soaked wood in the smoker unit. Fill the water pan halfway for steaks and almost full for whole salmon. Start the unit about 10 minutes before placing the fish on the grill. Steaks 1 inch thick take about 30 minutes; large salmon will take several hours. Take care not to overcook. Test with a fork inside the cavity at the thickest part of the fish. The flesh should flake easily.

If you have a large quantity of salmon, chill and freeze smoked salmon for future meals. It can be served cold or heated gently in a microwave oven.

SMOKED KING CRAB LEGS

Yield: 6 main dish or 12 appetizer servings
Heat Control: high, water pan ½ full

Serve this as an appetizer or entrée.

¼ cup melted butter
2 tablespoons white wine
1 tablespoon lemon juice
3 pounds thawed frozen Alaskan king crab legs

Combine the melted butter, wine, and lemon juice. Put the water pan in place and fill about ½ full with hot water. Generously brush the crab legs with the butter mixture. Set the cooking grill in place. Arrange the crab legs on the cooking grill. Cover. Smoke-cook about 1 hour, or until the crab meat is white and firm. You may wish to make additional basting sauce. It makes a marvelous dipping sauce.

SMOKED SHRIMP ON THE GRILL

Yield: 3 entrée servings, 6 appetizer servings

Heat Control: low, lid closed, indirect

These shrimp pick up a delightful smoked flavor and are especially good as hors d'oeuvres.

- 1 pound medium-sized shrimp, shelled
- ¼ pound butter
- 2 tablespoons lemon juice

Shell the shrimp. (This part can be done ahead of time.) Arrange the shrimp on a large piece of heavy-duty foil that will fit on the grill. To make the sauce, melt the butter and add fresh lemon juice. Generously brush the sauce over the shrimp. Place a foil packet of soaked hickory or fruitwood on the briquets according to the directions in the beginning of this chapter. Close the lid and smoke for about 10–15 minutes on low.

Shrimp should be eaten very soon after being smoked. If made in advance and chilled, serve with Seafood Cocktail Sauce (see recipe).

BAKED GARLIC TROUT

Yield: 4 servings

Heat Control: high, water pan ½ full

A nice easy way to prepare fresh trout with herbs.

- 2 whole cleaned trout (or any other white fish)
- Salt and pepper to taste
- ½ stick butter, softened
- ¼ clove garlic, crushed
- 1 tablespoon minced parsley
- 1 teaspoon minced onion
- ¼ cup white wine
- 1 tablespoon lemon juice
- Chopped parsley for garnish

Sprinkle the trout with salt and pepper. Set aside. Cream together the next four ingredients. Spread half of the mixture inside the cavity of each trout. Put the fish into a shallow baking dish. Combine the wine and lemon juice and pour over the trout. Put the water pan in place and fill about ½ full with hot water. Place baking dish on the grill and smoke for approximately 1 hour. Spoon the remaining juices in the pan over the fish and serve garnished with chopped parsley.

VEGETABLES

SMOKED MUSHROOMS

Yield: 4 servings

Heat Control: high, water pan at least ½ full

Serve with smoked beef, poultry, or fish. You'll love the smoky flavor that permeates these mushrooms.

- 1 pound large fresh mushrooms
- ¼ teaspoon garlic salt
- ¼ cup butter
- 2 tablespoons chopped parsley

Wash and drain mushrooms. Cut off only the tip of the stem. Butter a foil tray or shallow metal pan with the remaining butter, then arrange the mushrooms in the pan. Generously sprinkle with garlic salt and dot with most of the butter. Make sure the water pan is at least ½ full. Place the pan on the cooking grill along with the main dish for the last 45 minutes to an hour of cooking time. Do not slice the mushrooms.

SMOKED SPANISH ONIONS

Yield: 6 servings
Heat Control: high, water pan at least ½ full

A delicious accompaniment for your smoked meat—onions are crunchy, moist, and very flavorful.

2 large sweet onions, peeled
¼ cup melted butter
½ teaspoon salt
⅛ teaspoon pepper
¼ teaspoon beef bouillon granules

Slice the onions crosswise, ½ inch thick. Generously butter a shallow pan or a tray made from heavy-duty foil. Arrange the onion slices in the pan and brush with the ¼ cup of melted butter. Sprinkle with salt, pepper, and beef bouillon granules. Add to the cooking grill along with meat for the last 2–2½ hours of cooking time.

SMOKED CORN IN HUSKS

Yield: 1–2 ears per person (corn lovers have been known to eat 3–4 ears)
Heat Control: high, water pan ½ full

Wet husks wrapped around ears of corn prevent them from drying out.

Tender sweet corn in husks
Melted butter
Salt and pepper to taste, or seasoned salt, or lemon pepper

Pull the husks back from an ear of corn and remove the silk. Rinse the corn with water. Brush the ears with melted butter. Sprinkle with salt and pepper, seasoned salt, or lemon pepper. Replace the husks; leave an opening so the corn will be exposed to smoke. Fill water pan ½ full. Smoke 1½–2 hours, depending on the size and tenderness of corn. Corn will have a pleasant smoke flavor.

DILLY BAKED POTATOES

Yield: 3–4 servings
Heat Control: high, water pan almost full

Add these potatoes during the last 1½ hours when smoking a roast.

3 white potatoes, scrubbed and peeled
½ teaspoon dried dill
1 onion, sliced
Salt and pepper
Butter
Water

Slice the potatoes ½–¾ inch thick. Place on a double piece of heavy-duty aluminum foil. Sprinkle the bottom of the foil with some of the dill before placing the sliced potatoes on it. Place slices of onion between potato slices. Sprinkle generously with dill and add salt and pepper to taste and a dab of butter. Sprinkle with water. Wrap tightly. Fill water pan almost full. Place on the smoker grill and cook on high for 1½ hours. Turn the packets once during cooking time.

WATER PAN POTATOES

Yield: 1 potato per person
Heat Control: high, water to cover

Cook potatoes in the water pan during the last hour of smoking some other dish. Surprisingly, unpeeled potatoes pick up more flavor from drippings in the pan than peeled potatoes.

Small to medium red-skinned potatoes

Peel the potatoes or leave the skins on. Cooking time is the same for peeled and unpeeled potatoes. Scrub the potatoes well if cooking with the skins on. Add the potatoes to the water pan for the last hour of smoke-cooking. Water should cover the potatoes.

BAKED ZUCCHINI

Yield: ½ zucchini per person
Heat Control: high, water pan almost full

These zucchini can be smoked together with a number of different things.

Baby zucchini or yellow squash, about 6–8 inches long
Softened butter or margarine
Salt and seasoned pepper
Freshly grated Parmesan cheese

Wash the zucchini or squash well and cut in half lengthwise. Prick each half deeply with a fork on the cut side and score if desired. Spread with butter and sprinkle with salt and seasoned pepper. Sprinkle heavily with Parmesan cheese. Place in a large shallow pan or on a sheet of heavy foil with a little water in the bottom of the pan or foil. Fill water pan almost full. Smoke on the grill for 1 hour for a crunchy texture and 1½ hours for a softer texture. If the smoked flavor is not desired, cover with foil and follow the above directions.

SNACKS

SMOKED ALMONDS AND PECANS

Yield: about 12 ounces
Heat Control: high, water pan ½ full

Make these delicious munchies in large quantities. Serve as appetizer with beverages. They also make nice gifts.

5½ **ounces raw almonds**
5½ **ounces raw pecans**
1 **teaspoon seasoned salt**
¼ **teaspoon garlic powder**
¼ **teaspoon onion powder**
4 **drops of red pepper sauce**
1 **tablespoon Worcestershire sauce**
1 **tablespoon cooking oil**

Mix the almonds and pecans, salt, and powders. Then add the red pepper sauce, Worcestershire sauce, and oil. Fill water pan ½ full. Place nuts in a pie tin and smoke at a low temperature for 2 hours. Stir twice.

SMOKED CHEESE

Yield: 8 ounces
Heat Control: high, without water

An unusual and delicious treat. Make several batches at once, because this will keep, refrigerated, for up to 2 weeks. This smoked cheese is dry-smoked; do not use a water pan.

1 **8-ounce package Monterey Jack, Colby, muenster, or cream cheese**

Soak 2 or 3 chunks of wood. Make a shallow tray of several layers of heavy-duty foil or use a shallow foil pan. Poke holes in the foil or foil pan. If the cheese is not in slab shape, cut it into large chunks no thicker than 1 inch and arrange the chunks on the foil or pan. Add the wet wood to the smoker unit. Put the grill in place and set the cheese on the grill. The cheese will melt around the edges. Watch carefully, as you do not want cheese to become liquid or to boil, since that may toughen it. If the cheese is melting too fast, reduce the heat to medium. Cover and smoke-flavor the cheese for 45 minutes to 1 hour, depending on type of cheese, or until the cheese is richly browned and flavored. Check at intervals to make sure the cheese is not melting excessively. Serve the cheese while it is still warm or let it cool slightly and then wrap it tightly in plastic wrap and chill. Let the chilled cheese stand at room temperature about an hour before serving or heat in a microwave oven until soft. Serve with crackers or dip fresh vegetables into the hot melted cheese. Monterey Jack is especially good this way.

Appendix:
Party Calculator

Most people can handle party foods and drinks for up to 10 guests without big problems. This party calculator for 10 people can be easily multiplied for groups of 20, 30, 50, and more. Here are some tips to ensure the success of any party.

- Plan all aspects of the party—menu, preparation, service, decoration, music, cleanup, etc.—well ahead of time and write them down.
- Select the menu only after considering if it can be properly prepared, stored, and served with ease (cold things cold, hot items hot, etc.).
- Use Charmglow's Party Calculator Chart, which follows, when writing up your shopping list and menu recipes.
- Get plenty of help for food preparation, serving, and cleanup. Assign duties and schedules.
- Be sure to have adequate cooking pans, utensils, serving trays, etc., both in size and in quantity. If you don't have the proper equipment, you can rent or borrow.
- Advance preparation is important. Many foods can be partially cooked and require only heating or garnishing at serving time. Some foods, such as soups, chowders, casseroles, and all kinds of dessert, can be fully prepared and frozen weeks in advance of your party. Have deli foods sliced.
- Set up the serving area in advance and make a dry run with empty platters, etc., checking arrangements for ease of serving and traffic flow. If self-service, plan traffic down both sides of the serving table.
- Arrange main courses only at the main serving table. Have bread, condiments, coffee, and beverages at separate tables, away from the main serving area.
- If disposable plates, etc., are used, buy top-quality, heavy-duty types for eating convenience and to avoid accidents.
- Prewrap table utensils in paper napkins.
- Have plenty of extra napkins, ashtrays, and waste containers set at convenient spots.
- Chill wines or beverages in new plastic trash barrels filled with crushed ice to save refrigerator space for food. Set containers in the serving area.
- Arrange food just prior to serving and plan to refill the buffet as needed during the party, instead of putting all the food out at once.
- Decorate the serving and entertaining areas with seasonal fresh fruits and/or flowers, as well as candles or other outdoor lighting.
- Foods that require portion control during serving should be attended, especially for large parties. Smaller groups may be allowed to slice their own meats or cheese if it doesn't slow up service.
- Be sure to allow adequate room for guests to eat, whether standing or sitting.

- Avoid congestion and put away any breakable valuables to ensure against accidents.
- Plan up to three hours for eating and conversation. The party may be ended by serving dessert and coffee and/or by closing down the wine or beverage service.
- Let others do the serving and cleanup. Mingle with your guests and enjoy your own party!

Charmglow Party Calculator Chart
(For 10 Servings)

	SERVING PER PERSON	AMOUNT TO BUY OR PREPARE
BEVERAGES		
Champagne or wine punch	4-oz. cup	5 cups
Fruit drink or punch	6-oz. glass	7½ cups
Coffee (regular)	1½ cups	⅔ cup
		15 cups water
Tea	1½ cups	5 tea bags
		15 cups water
Cocoa	1 cup	¾ cup cocoa
		2½ qts. milk or liquid
		1¼ cups sugar
		1½ teaspoons vanilla
Dinner Wine	6–12 oz.	2½ to 5 bottles (750ml each)
Dessert Wine	4–5 oz.	1½ to 2 bottles (750ml each)
BREADS AND ROLLS		
Bread (1-pound loaf)	1–2 slices	1 loaf
Rolls	1½–2	1½ dozen
MEATS		
Beef		
Ground (for hamburgers)	4 oz.	2½ lbs.
Roast (boneless)	3 oz.	2 lbs.
Roast (bone in)	8 oz.	5 lbs.
Steak (boneless)	4 oz.	3 lbs.
Steak (bone in)	5 oz.	4 lbs.
Stew (vegetable recipe)	3 oz. meat	3 lbs.
Lamb		
Chops	2 chops	5 lbs.
Roast (boneless)	3 oz.	3 lbs.
Roast (bone in)	3 oz.	5 lbs.
Pork (fresh)		
Chops	2 chops	4–5 lbs.
Roast (boneless)	3 oz.	4 lbs.
Roast (bone in)	3 oz.	5 lbs.

	SERVING PER PERSON	AMOUNT TO BUY OR PREPARE
Sausage (bulk or link)	3 oz.	3 lbs.
Spareribs	6 oz.	5 lbs.
Pork (cured)		
Bacon	2 slices	2 lbs.
Ham (uncooked bone in)	3 oz.	5 lbs.
Ham (uncooked boneless)	3 oz.	3 lbs.
Ham (fully cooked boneless)	3 oz.	2¼ lbs.
Ham (canned)	3 oz.	2¼ lbs.
Miscellaneous		
Cold cuts	2 oz.	1¼ lbs.
Frankfurters (10 to 1 lb.)	2 or 1½ oz.	2 lbs.
Meatloaf	3 oz.	4 lbs.

FISH AND SEAFOOD

Shrimp (shelled)	4 oz.	2½ lbs.
Lobster or crab (in shell)	8 oz.	5 lbs.
Fish steaks or fillets	5 oz.	3½ lbs.

POULTRY

Chicken		
Broilers	half	5
Fryers (cut up)	8 oz.	5
Boneless meat for recipe	3 oz.	2 lbs.
Turkey		
Whole	4 oz. edible	5–6 lbs.
Rolled roasted (boneless)	4 oz.	3½ lbs.

VEGETABLES

Frozen	½ cup	2 lbs.
Canned	½ cup	2½-lb. cans
Potatoes (baked)	1 med.	4 lbs.
Potatoes (creamed or scalloped)	½ cup	2 lbs.
Potatoes (mashed)	½ cup	3 lbs.
Lettuce (garnish or cups)	10 per head	1 head
Lettuce (mixed green salad)	6 per head	1½ heads
Tomatoes (sliced)	4 slices	2 lbs.
Carrots, celery, etc. (sticks)	3 oz.	2 lbs.
Parsley, watercress (garnish)	1 sprig	1 bunch
Radishes	2–3	1 bunch

FRUITS

Fresh (sectioned and pared)	½ cup	2 lbs.
Grapes (fresh bunches)	½ cup	2 lbs.
Melon (cantaloupe, etc.)	half	5
Melon (watermelon)	1" thick slice	10 lbs.
Canned	½ cup	2½-lb. cans

Appendix: Party Calculator

	SERVING PER PERSON	AMOUNT TO BUY OR PREPARE
DESSERTS		
Cake (2 10-inch layers, 14 pieces)	1 piece	1 cake
Pie (9-inch, 6 cuts)	1 piece	1½ pies
Ice Cream—sherbert	½ cup	½ gallon
DAIRY PRODUCTS		
Milk	8 oz.	2½ qts.
Butter pats (48 per lb.)	1–1½ pats	¼ lb.
Butter (for vegetables)	1 tsp.	2½ T.
Cream (for coffee)	1 T.	½ cup plus 2 T.
Cream (whipped for dessert)	2 T.	1¼ cups
Eggs (hard-cooked for sandwiches)	1	1 dozen
Eggs (scrambled)	½ cup	1¼ dozen
CONDIMENTS		
Ketchup, mustard, relish	½–1 T.	½ cup
Jam, Jelly	1½–2 T.	1 cup
Pickles	1 medium	1 pt.
Mayonnaise	1½ T.	1 cup
Peanut butter or sandwich filling	2 T.	1-lb. jar
Salad dressing (liquid)	1 T.	⅔ cup
PREPARED FOODS		
Potato or macaroni salad	½ cup	3 lbs.
Baked beans	½ cup	2½ lbs.
Spaghetti-macaroni (uncooked)	1½ cups	2 lbs.
Spaghetti sauce	½ cup	5 cups
Gravy (for meats)	2 T.	⅔ cup
Dressing (bread or rice)	½ cup	5 cups
Rice	⅔ cup	2 cups rice/4½ cups water

Index

A

Acorn Squash with Apples, 82
Alfredo, Noodles, 114
All-American Hot Dog, 94
Almonds and Pecans, Smoked, 136
Angels on Horseback, 28
Appetizers, 25–32
   adapting your favorite recipes for barbecue cooking, 26
   Angels on Horseback, 28
   Beef Jerky, 123
   Beef Roll-Ups, 27
   Cha Shui (Chinese Pork Appetizers), 30
   Cheese Crispies, 28–29
   Chinese Hot Mustard Sauce, 23
   Chinese Spareribs with Black-Bean Sauce, 31
   Deviled Hamburger on French Bread, 93
   Fast Indian saté, 53
   Hawaiian Bamboo Beef Appetizers, 29
   Hot Swiss Bacon Sandwich Loaf, 98
   Kraut and Bacon Stuffed Barbecued Sausages, 96
   Lemon Scampi, 74
   Minced Pigeon (Chicken Breasts), 111
   Pheasant (Smoked), 128
   Pineapple Pork Teriyaki, 32
   Pork Strips with Hot Mustard, 27
   Rumaki, 27
   Shrimp 'N' Dill Appetizer, 28
   Smoked Almonds and Pecans, 136
   Smoked Cheese, 136–37
   Smoked King Crab Legs, 133
   Smoked Mushrooms, 134–35
   Smoked Shrimp, 134
   Stuffed Mushrooms, 29
   Teriyaki Chicken Wings, 31
   White Fish Mousse, 132–33
Apple Pie Brownies, 105
Apples. *See* Acorn Squash with Apples
Apples, Spiced, 86
Armenian Chicken, 60
Asparagus in Wok, Fresh, 114
Asparagus with Lemon Butter, 82

B

Baby Back Ribs (Smoked), 127
Back Ribs, Lemon-Dill (Smoked), 127
Bacon Burgers, 92
Bacon and Cheese, Potatoes Baked in Foil, 85
Bacon Sandwich Loaf, Hot Swiss, 98
Bacon Stuffed Barbecued Sausages, and Kraut, 96
Baked Garlic Trout (Smoked), 134
Baked Potatoes, 84–85
Baked Potatoes in Foil with Bacon and Cheese, 85
Baked Zucchini (Smoked), 136
Bananas Flambé, 86–87
Barbecue Roasted Chicken or Capon, 58
Barbecue Sauce for Oriental Spareribs, 19
Barbecue Scramble, 113
Barbecued Pork Roast, Smoked, 125
Barbecued Ribs, 48–49
Barbecued Swordfish, 69
Bar-B-Q-Sauce, Charmglow, 19
Basic Grilled Hamburgers, 90–91
Basic Poultry Marinade, 20
Basted Garden Vegetables, 83
Basting Sauce, Ginger, 21
Basting Sauce, Pork, 20
Basting Sauce, Sweet and Sour, 21
Bavarian Ribs and Kraut (Smoked), 126–27
Bean Pot, Chuck Wagon, 80
Bean Sprouts, Stir-Fried, 114–15
Beans, Boston Baked, 81
Beans, Bourbon Baked, 81
Beans, Green 'N' Mushrooms, 79
Beans, Zesty Baked, 81
Bearnaise Sauce, 24
Beef, 34–44
Beef appetizers, Hawaiian Bamboo, 29
Beef Jerky, 123
Beef, Mongolian, 112–13
Beef Roast, Rolled Boneless, 43
Beef roasts for spit and grill, 37
Beef Roll-Ups, 27
Beef Short Ribs, Herbed, 124
Beets, Buttered, 79
Benefits of gas grilling, 12–14
   gas pays off again and again, 13–14
Best Hamburger Ever, 93
Biscuits, Refrigerated, 104
Black-bean sauce, with Chinese spareribs, 31
Bohemian Pork Roast (Smoked), 126
Boneless Ham, 52
Boston Baked Beans, 81
Bourbon Baked Beans, 80
Brats in Beer Wisconsin-Style, 96
Brat-Wiches, German Grilled, 95
Breads, 101–5
   Brown-and-Serve Rolls on a Spit, 101
   Cheese-stuffed French Rolls, 103
   Cinnamon French Toast, 104–105
   Deviled Hamburger on French Bread, 93
   Frozen Bread, 102
   Garlic Bread, 102
   Onion-Cheese loaf, 103
   Refrigerated Biscuits, 104
   Roquefort Bread, 103
   Sourdough Meat Loaf, 97
Brisket of Corned Beef, Roast, 44
Broiled Halibut, Japanese, 70
Brown-and-Serve Rolls on a Spit, 101
Brown Butter Sauce, 24
Brownies, Apple Pie, 105
Buns, Shrimp, 99
Burgers, Bacon, 92
Burgers, Mexican, 93
Burgers, Mushroom, 92
Burgers, Oriental, 94
Burgers, Stroganoff, 94

Index

Butt Steak with Vinaigrette Lettuce, 38
Butter Sauce, Brown, 24
Butter Sauce, Lemon, 82
Buttered Beets, 79

C

Capon or Chicken, Barbecue Roasted, 58
Carrots, Dilled, 83
Cauliflower, Steamed, 79
Cha Shui (Chinese Pork Appetizers), 30
Charmglow Bar-B-Q-Sauce, 19
Charmglow Basket Chicken, 58
Charmglow Marinade for Steaks, 19
Charmglow marinade with sirloin steak, 42-43
Charmglow party calculator for 10 people, 139-43
Cheddar Dogs, 94-95
Cheese and bacon with potatoes baked in foil, 85
Cheese Burgers, Hot Ham 'N, 99
Cheeseburgers, Deluxe, 92
Cheese Crispies, 28-29
Cheese-Onion Loaf, 103
Cheese Sandwiches and Flank Steak, 101
Cheese, Smoked, 136-37
Cheese-stuffed French Rolls, 103
Cherries Jubilee, 115
Chicken, Armenian, 60
Chicken Breasts. See Minced Pigeon
Chicken Breasts, Chinese, 30-31
Chicken, Charmglow Basket, 58
Chicken Chow Mein, 112
Chicken Epicurean (Stuffed Chicken), 59
Chicken in Foil, Delectable, 59
Chicken Legs, Sassy, 61
Chicken Livers. See Rumaki
Chicken or Capon, Barbecue Roasted, 58
Chicken Shashlik, 58-59
Chicken, Smoked Whole, 131
Chicken Teriyaki, Smoked, 132
Chicken/Turkey Patties, 61
Chicken with Dry Red Pepper, 110
Chinese Grilled Halibut, 70-71
Chinese Hot Mustard Sauce, 23
Chinese Chicken Breasts, 30-31
Chinese Spareribs with Black-Bean Sauce, 31
Chopped Sirloin with Green Onion, 39
Chopped Steak, Luau, 52-53
Chow Mein, Chicken, 112
Chuck Roast, "Meal-in-One", 43
Chuck Wagon Bean Pot, 80
Chuck Wagon Steak, 39
Cinnamon French Toast, 104-105
Clam Bake, New England, 75
Cocktail Sauce, Seafood, 23
Cooking with foil, 8
Corn in Foil, 84
Corn in Husks, Smoked, 135
Crispies, Cheese, 28-29
Crispy Corn Pone, 104

Corn Roasted in the Husk, 84
Corned Beef, Roast Brisket of, 44
Corned Beef, Smoked, 123
Crab Legs, Smoked King, 133
Crab Stuffing, Trout with, 69
Crown Roast of Lamb, 46

D

Delectable Chicken in Foil, 59
Deluxe Cheeseburgers, 92
Derby Pie, Kentucky, 105
Desserts
    Applie Pie Brownies, 105
    Bananas Flambé, 86-87
    Cherries Jubilee, 115
    Grilled Pears, 86
    Kentucky Derby Pie, 105
    Spiced Apples, 86
Deviled Hamburger on French Bread, 93
Dill Appetizer, Shrimp 'N', 28
Dilled Carrots, 83
Dilly Baked Potatoes (Smoked), 135
Dipping Sauce, Soy, 23
Dipping Sauce, Sweet and Sour, 23
Dogs, Cheddar, 94-95
Dogs, Reuben, 95
Dressing. See also Roast Leg of Lamb with Herb Stuffing
    Turkey Wings with (Smoked), 130
    Wild Rice, 45
Duck with Orange Sauce, Smoked, 130-31
Duck with Orange Sauce, Wild (Smoked), 131

E

East Indian Saté, 53
Eggplant El Greco, 80
Eggs, scrambled. See Barbecue Scramble
El Greco, Eggplant, 80
Extra-Special Barbecued Spareribs (Smoked), 128

F

Fish Fillets in Lemon Butter, 70
Fish, Foil-Wrapped, 72
Fish Mousse, White (Smoked), 132-33
Fish, Pan, 132
Fish and Seafood, 65-75
    chart, 67-68
    cooking, 66-67
    shellfish, 66-67
Fish, Soy Sauce for Barbecued, 20
Flambe, Bananas, 86-87
Flank Steak and Cheese Sandwiches, 101
Flank Steak, Pungent Smoky, 122
Foil-Wrapped Fish, 72
French Bread, Deviled Hamburger on, 93
French Rolls, Cheese-Stuffed, 103
French Toast, Cinnamon, 104-105

Fresh Asparagus in Wok, 114
Fresh Grilled Tomatoes, 83
Frozen Bread, 102
Fruit-Roasted Pheasant (Smoked), 128
Fruits
    Acorn Squash with Apples, 82
    Apple Pie Brownies, 105
    Bananas Flambe, 86-87
    Cherries Jubilee, 115
    Fruit-Roasted Pheasant (Smoked), 128
    Grilled Pears, 86
    Pineapple Pork Teriyaki, 32
    Spiced Apples, 86
Fruits and vegetables, 77-87

G

Game Hens, Orange-Ginger, 60
Game Marinade, Wild, 21
Garlic Bread, 102
Gas grilling charts
    fish and seafood, 67-68
    hamburger, 91
    meats, 4-6
    potatoes, 85
    poultry, 7
    ribs, 48
    sausage, 90
Gaucho Thick Steak, 41
Ginger Basting Sauce, 21
Green Beans 'N' Mushrooms, 79
Grilled German Brat-Wiches, 95
Grilled Minute Steak, 42
Grilled Pears, 86
Grilled Pork Chops, 50
Grilled Salmon, 72
Grilled Salmon Patties, 71
Grilled Salmon with Tarragon Mayonnaise, 71
Grilled Veal Cutlet, 44

H

Halibut, Chinese Grilled, 70-71
Halibut, Japanese Broiled, 70
Ham, Boneless, 52
Ham 'N Cheese Burgers, 99
Ham, Spit Grilled, 52
Hamburger on French Bread, Deviled, 93
Hamburgers
    Bacon Burgers, 92
    Basic grilled hamburgers, 90-91
    Best Hamburger Ever, 93
    Deluxe Cheeseburgers, 92
    Deviled Hamburger on French Bread, 93
    Mexican Burgers, 93
    Mushroom Burgers, 92
    Oriental Burgers, 94
    Steve's Hamburgers, 92
    Stroganoff Burgers, 94

Hawaiian Bamboo Beef Appetizers, 29
Hen, Rock Cornish, 61
Herbed Beef Short Ribs, 124
Herbed Rock Cornish Hens, 60-61
Hot Dogs
    All-American Hot Dog, 94
    Cheddar Dogs, 94-95
    Reuben Dogs, 95
Hot Ham 'N Cheese Burgers, 99
Hot Mustard, Pork Strips with, 27
Hot Swiss Bacon Sandwich Loaf, 98
Hot Tuna Sandwiches, 99
How to cook with your gas grill, 1
    cooking methods, 4
    getting acquainted with your grill, 2;
        temperature chart for one-burner, 3;
        two-burner grill, 2

I

Indian Saté, East, 53
Irish Potatoes, 85
Italian Sausage (Mild or Hot), 96
Italian Steak Sandwiches, 100-101

J

Japanese Broiled Halibut, 70
Jerky, Beef, 123

K

Kentucky Derby Pie, 105
King Crab Legs, Smoked, 133
Kraut and Bacon Stuffed Barbecued Sausages, 96
Kraut, Bavarian Ribs and (Smoked), 126-27

L

Lamb, 45-47
Lamb Chops, 45
Lamb Chops, Mushroom-Stuffed, 47
Lamb cooking chart, 45
Lamb, Crown Roast of, 46
Lamb, Pita Bread Stuffed with, 97
Lamb Shish-Kabob, 47
Leg of Lamb with Herb Stuffing, Roast, 46-47
Lemon Butter Asparagus with, 82
Lemon Butter, Fish Fillets in, 70
Lemon Butter Sauce. See Asparagus with Lemon Butter
Lemon-Dill Back Ribs (Smoked), 127
Lemon Scampi, 74
Lettuce, Butt Steak, with Vinaigrette, 38
Lobster Tails on the Grill, 75
Low-calorie cooking, 13
Luau Chopped Steak, 52-53

M

Mandarin Pork, 50-51
Marinades and Sauces, 15-24
    Basic Poultry Marinade, 20
    Basted Garden Vegetables, 83
    Charmglow Marinade for Steaks, 19
    flavor, 16
    glazing, 17
    juiciness, 17
    other seasonings, 18
    seasoning the briquets, 18
    table seasoning, 17
    tenderness, 16
    the secret's in the sauce, 16
    Wild Game Marinade, 21
"Meal-In-One" Chuck Roast, 43
Meat Loaf in Foil, 44
Meat Loaf, Smoked, 122-23
Meat loaf, Sourdough, 97
Meats, 33-53
    beef steaks for barbecuing, 35
    frozen meats, 34
    gas grill meat chart, 4-6
    roast cooking tips, 35
    steak cooking tips, 34
Mexican Burgers, 93
Microwave, 9
    barbecue for meals ahead, 10
    pairing a microwave with your gas grill, 9
Minced Pigeon (Chicken Breasts), 111
Minute Steak, Grilled, 42
Mongolian Beef, 112-13
Muffins. *See* Crispy Corn Pone
Mushroom Brochette, Shrimp and, 74
Mushroom Burgers, 92
Mushrooms in Foil, 82
Mushrooms 'N' Green Beans, 79
Mushrooms, Smoked, 134-35
Mushrooms, Stuffed, 29
Mushroom-Stuffed Lamb Chops, 47
Mustard Sauce, Chinese Hot, 23

N

Nacho Sandwiches, 98
New England Clam Bake, 75
Noodles Alfredo, 114
Noodles in Wok, Rice, 113

O

Onion-Cheese Loaf, 103
Onion Kisses, 84
Onions, Spanish Smoked, 135
Orange-Ginger Game Hens, 60
Oriental Burgers, 94
Oriental Shrimp on a Skewer, 73
Oriental Spareribs, 48
Oriental Turkey Legs (Smoked), 130
Oysters. *See* Angels on Horseback

P

Pan Fish (Smoked), 132
Party calculator for 10 people, 139-43
Patties
    Grilled Salmon, 71
    Romano Veal, 45
    Turkey/Chicken, 61
Pears, Grilled, 86
Pecans, Smoked Almonds and, 136
Pepper Steak Flambe. *See* Steak Au Poivre
Pheasant, Fruit-Roasted (Smoked), 128
Pheasant (Smoked), 128
Pie, Apple Brownies, 105
Pie, Kentucky Derby, 105
Pineapple Pork Teriyaki, 32
Pita Bread Stuffed with Lamb, 97
Pork Basting Sauce, 20
Pork Chops, Grilled, 50
Pork Chops, Smoked, 50
Pork Chops, Stuffed (Smoked), 125
Pork cookery, 47-52
Pork, Mandarin, 50-51
Pork Roast, Bohemian (Smoked), 126
Pork Roast, Rolled, 51
Pork Roast (Smoked), 126
Pork Roast, Smoked Barbecued, 125
Pork Roast, Spit-Roasted Rolled, 50
Pork Sirloin Roast, 51
Pork Strips with Hot Mustard, 27
Pork Tenderloin. *See* Cha Shui (Chinese Pork Appetizers)
Pork Teriyaki, Pineapple, 32
Potato cooking chart, 85
Potatoes, Baked, 84-85
Potatoes Baked in Foil with Bacon and Cheese, 85
Potatoes, Dilly Baked (Smoked), 135
Potatoes, Irish, 85
Potatoes, Water Pan (Smoked), 136
Poultry, 55-64
    chicken, 56-57
    cornish hens, 56-57
    game birds, 56-57
    turkey, 56-57
Poultry Marinade, Basic, 20
Pungent Smoky Flank Steak, 122

R

Rainbow Trout, 73
Rancho Grande Steak, 38-39
Red Snapper, Shanghai Grilled, 72
Refrigerated Biscuits, 104
Reuben Dogs, 95
Ribs and Kraut, Bavarian (Smoked), 126-27
Ribs, Baby Back (Smoked), 127

Ribs, Barbecued, 48–49
Ribs cooking chart, 6, 48
Ribs, Lemon-Dill Back (Smoked), 127
Rice Dressing, Wild, 45
Rice Noodles in Wok, 113
Roast Brisket of Corned Beef, 44
Roast Leg of Lamb with Herb Stuffing, 46–47
Roast of Lamb, Crown, 46
Roasted Corn in the Husk, 84
Roasted Turkey, 62
Roasted Turkey, Stuffed, 62–63
Rock Cornish Hen, 61
Rock Cornish Hens, Herbed, 60–61
Rolled Boneless Beef Roast, 43
Rolled Pork Roast, 51
Rolled Pork Roast, Spit-Roasted, 50
Rolled Sirloin Tip (Italian Style) (Smoked), 122
Rolls. See Breads
Rolls on a Spit, Brown-and-Serve, 101
Roll-Ups, Beef, 27
Romano Veal Patties, 45
Roquefort Bread, 103
Roquefort Sauce for Steak, 20
Rotisserie cooking, 10
    arranging meat on your spit, 10
    drip pans, 10
    grilling method, 10
    meat thermometer, 11
    poultry rotisserie, 11
    rotisserie basket, 11
    rotisserie motor, 11
    uneven balancing, 10
Round Steak in Foil, 40
Rum Steak, 42
Rumaki, 27

S

Salads
    Butt Steak with Vinaigrette Lettuce, 38
    Wilted Spinach, 115
Salisbury Steaks with Roquefort, 42
Salmon, Grilled, 72
Salmon Patties, Grilled, 71
Salmon, Smoked, 133
Salmon with Tarragon Mayonnaise, Grilled, 71
Sandwich Loaf, Hot Swiss Bacon, 98
Sandwiches
    Flank Steak and Cheese, 101
    Hot Ham 'N Cheese Burgers, 99
    Hot Tuna Sandwiches, 99
    Italian Steak, 100–101
    Nacho, 98
    Pita Bread Stuffed wth Lamb, 97
    Rancho Grande Steak, 38–39
    Shrimp Buns, 99
    Stroganoff Steak, 100
    Swiss Tuna Grill, 100
Sassy Chicken Legs, 61

Sauces
    Barbecue Sauce for Oriental Spareribs, 19
    Bearnaise, 24
    Brown Butter, 24
    Charmglow Bar-B-Q, 19
    Chinese Hot Mustard, 23
    Ginger Basting, 21
    Lemon butter with asparagus, 82
    Pork Basting, 20
    Roquefort Sauce for Steak, 20
    Seafood Cocktail, 23
    Smoked Duck with Orange Sauce, 130–31
    Soy Dipping, 23
    Soy Sauce for Barbecued Fish, 20
    Sweet and Sour Basting, 21
    Sweet and Sour Dipping, 23
    Sweet and Sour Table, 24
    Tarragon Mayonnaise with Grilled Salmon, 71
    Tomato, 21
Sausage cooking chart, 90
Sausage, Italian (Mild or Hot), 96
Sausage without Casing, smoked, 124–25
Scallops in Shells, 74–75
Scampi, lemon, 74
Scrambled eggs. See Barbecue Scramble
Seafood Cocktail Sauce, 23
Seafood and fish, 65–75
Shanghai Grilled Red Snapper, 72
Shashlik, Chicken, 58–59
Shells, Scallops in, 74–75
Shish-Kabob, Lamb, 47
Short Ribs, Herbed Beef (Smoked), 124
Shrimp and Mushroom Brochette, 74
Shrimp Buns, 99
Shrimp in the Wok, 110
Shrimp 'N' Dill Appetizer, 28
Shrimp on a Skewer, Oriental, 73
Shrimp on the Grill, Smoked, 134
Sirloin, Chopped with Green Onion, 39
Sirloin Roast, Pork, 51
Sirloin Steak with Charmglow Marinade, 42–43
Sirloin Tip, Rolled (Italian Style) (Smoked), 122
Skewered Vegetables. See Basted Garden Vegetables
Smoke cooking with a water smoker, 118–120
    cleaning your water smoker, 120
    flavoring the meat, 120
    opening and closing your water smoker, 119–20
    timing, 119
    water pan, 119
Smoked Almonds and Pecans, 136
Smoked Barbecued Pork Roast, 125
Smoked Cheese, 136–37
Smoked Chicken Teriyaki, 132
Smoked Corn in Husks, 135
Smoked Corned Beef, 123
Smoked Duck with Orange Sauce, 130–131
Smoked King Crab Legs, 133
Smoked Meat Loaf, 122–23
Smoked Mushrooms, 134–35

Index

Smoked Pork Chops, 50
Smoked Salmon, 133
Smoked Sausage without Casing, 124–25
Smoked Shrimp on the Grill, 134
Smoked Spanish Onions, 135
Smoked Turkey Breast, 129
Smoked Turkey Breast, Ultimate, 129
Smoked Whole Chicken, 131
Smoked Whole Turkey, 129
Smoker cooking, 117–137
   cooking chart, 120–21
Snacks
   Smoked Almonds and Pecans, 136
   Smoked Cheese, 136–37
Sourdough Meat Loaf, 97
Soy Dipping Sauce, 23
Soy Sauce for Barbecued Fish, 20
Spareribs (Smoked), 127
Spareribs, Barbecue Sauce for Oriental, 19
Spareribs, Extra Special Barbecued (Smoked), 128
Spareribs on a Spit, 49
Spareribs, Oriental, 48
Spareribs with Black-Bean Sauce, Chinese, 31
Spiced Apples, 86
Spinach Salad, Wilted, 115
Spit-grilled Ham, 52
Spit-Roasted Rolled Pork Roast, 50
Spit, Spareribs on a, 49
Squash, Acorn with Apples, 82
Steak and Cheese Sandwiches, Flank, 101
Steak Au Poivre (Pepper Steak Flambe), 40
Steak, Butt, with Vinaigrette Lettuce, 38
Steak, Chuck Wagon, 39
Steak, Gaucho Thick, 41
Steak, Grilled Minute, 42
Steak in Foil, Round, 40
Steak, Luau Chopped, 52–53
Steak Packet Dinner, Swiss, 40–41
Steak, Pungent Smoky Flank, 122
Steak, Rancho Grande, 38–39
Steak, Roquefort Sauce for, 20
Steak Sandwiches, Italian, 100–101
Steak Sandwich, Stroganoff, 100
Steak, Sirloin, with Charmglow Marinade, 42–43
Steak, Rum, 42
Steaks, Charmglow Marinade for, 19
Steaks, Salisbury with Roquefort, 42
Steamed Cauliflower, 79
Steve's Hamburgers, 92
Stir-Fried Bean Sprouts, 114–15
Stroganoff Burgers, 94
Stroganoff Steak Sandwich, 100
Stuffed Chicken. See Chicken Epicurean
Stuffed Mushrooms, 29
Stuffed Pork Chops (Smoked), 125
Stuffed Roasted Turkey, 62–63
Stuffed Zucchini, 81
Stuffing
   Mushroom-stuffed Lamb Chops, 47
   Roast Leg of Lamb with Herb Stuffing, 46–47
   Stuffed Pork Chops (Smoked), 125
   stuffing chart, 62
   Turkey Wings with Dressing (Smoked), 130
   Wild Rice Dressing, 45
Sweet and Sour Basting Sauce, 21
Sweet and Sour Dipping Sauce, 23
Sweet and Sour Table Sauce, 24
Swiss Bacon Sandwich Loaf, Hot, 98
Swiss Steak Packet Dinner, 40–41
Swiss Tuna Grill, 100
Swordfish, Barbecued, 69

T

Table Sauce, Sweet and Sour, 24
Tarragon Mayonnaise, Grilled Salmon with, 71
Teriyaki Chicken Wings, 31
Teriyaki, Smoked Chicken, 132
Toast, Cinnamon French, 104–105
Tomato Sauce, 21
Tomatoes, Fresh Grilled, 83
Top Round Steak. See Rancho Grande Steak
Tortillas. See Cheese Crispies
Troubleshooting your grill, 11
   cooking temperatures, 11
   flare-up, 12
   heat variations, 12
Trout, Baked Garlic (Smoked), 134
Trout, Rainbow, 73
Trout with Crab Stuffing, 69
Tuna Grill, Swiss, 100
Tuna Sandwich Filling, Hot, 99
Turkey Breast, Smoked, 129
Turkey Breast, Ultimate Smoked, 129
Turkey/Chicken Patties, 61
Turkey Legs, Oriental (Smoked), 130
Turkey, Roasted, 62
Turkey, Smoked Whole, 129
Turkey, Stuffed Roasted, 62–63
Turkey Wings with Dressing (Smoked), 130
Turkeys, 61–64
   chart on stuffing, 62
   Split-Barbecue Turkey, 63–64

U

Ultimate Smoked Turkey Breast, 129

V

Veal, 44–45
Veal Cutlet, Grilled, 44
Veal Patties, Romano, 45
Vegetables
   Acorn Squash with Apples, 82
   Asparagus with Lemon Butter, 82
   Baked Potatoes, 84–85
   Baked Zucchini (Smoked), 136

Basted Garden Vegetables, 83
Bavarian Ribs and Kraut (Smoked), 126–27
Boston Baked Beans, 81
Bourbon Baked Beans, 80
Butt Steak with Vinaigrette Lettuce, 38
Buttered Beets, 79
Chuck Wagon Bean Pot, 80
Corn in Foil, 84
Corn Roasted in the Husk, 84
Dilled Carrots, 83
Dilly Baked Potatoes (Smoked), 135
Eggplant El Greco, 80
Fresh Asparagus in Wok, 114
Fresh Grilled Tomatoes, 83
Green Beans 'N' Mushrooms, 79
Irish Potatoes, 85
Mushrooms in Foil, 82
Onion Kisses, 84
Potatoes Baked in Foil with Bacon and Cheese, 85
Smoked Corn in Husks, 135
Smoked Mushrooms, 134–35
Smoked Spanish Onions, 135
Steamed Cauliflower, 79
Stir-Fried Bean Sprouts, 114–15
Stuffed Mushrooms, 29
Stuffed Zucchini, 81
Water Pan Potatoes (Smoked), 136
Wilted Spinach Salad, 115
Zesty Baked Beans, 81

W

Water Pan Potatoes (Smoked), 136
White Fish Mousse (Smoked), 132–33
Wild Duck with Orange Sauce (Smoked), 131
Wild Game Marinade, 21
Wild Rice Dressing, 45
Wilted Spinach Salad, 115
Wok cooking, 107–15
    choosing and caring for your wok, 108
    how to use a wok on a gas grill, 108
    steaming, 109
    stir-frying, 108–109

Z

Zesty Baked Beans, 81
Zucchini, Baked (Smoked), 136
Zucchini, Stuffed, 81